Spiritual Warfare

HOLY SPIRIT
ESSENTIALS

Spiritual Warfare

LEARN TO RECOGNIZE AND ENGAGE VICTORIOUSLY

DR. NEIL T. ANDERSON AND
DR. TIMOTHY M. WARNER

Chosen
a division of Baker Publishing Group
Minneapolis, Minnesota

© 2025 by Neil T. Anderson and Timothy M. Warner

Published by Chosen Books
Minneapolis, Minnesota
ChosenBooks.com

Chosen Books is a division of
Baker Publishing Group, Grand Rapids, Michigan

Previously published by Regal Books under the title *The Beginner's Guide to Spiritual Warfare*

Previously published by Bethany House Publishers under the title *The Essential Guide to Spiritual Warfare*

Library of Congress Cataloging-in-Publication Data

Names: Anderson, Neil T., author | Warner, Timothy M. author
Title: Spiritual warfare : learn to recognize and engage victoriously / Neil T. Anderson and Timothy M. Warner.
Other titles: Beginner's guide to spiritual warfare
Description: Minneapolis, Minnesota : Chosen, a division of Baker Publishing Group, 2025. | Series: Holy Spirit essentials | "Previously published by Regal Books under the title The Beginner's Guide to Spiritual Warfare. Second edition published by Chosen Books in 2016"—Title page verso.
Identifiers: LCCN 2025009395 | ISBN 9780800778347 paperback | ISBN 9780800778354 casebound | ISBN 9781493452316 ebook
Subjects: LCSH: Spiritual warfare
Classification: LCC BV4509.5 .A522 2025 | DDC 248.4—dc23/eng/20250609
LC record available at https://lccn.loc.gov/2025009395

CONTENTS

ONE

Welcome to the War!

As a boy, I (Tim) was not a fighter. I threw apples at the bullies, but most often I ran! Ninety days out of high school, however, I was drafted into the United States Army. I began learning to fight—and I hated fighting. I hated the idea of shooting another human. I hated practicing how to harm or kill with my hands. Stabbing a straw-filled dummy with a bayonet turned my stomach. I was a reluctant warrior. (In His mercy, God kindly found this reluctant warrior a place in the chaplain corps.)

A Reluctant Spiritual Warrior

I was a reluctant spiritual warrior, too. In the church where I grew up, I was taught to ignore Satan or demons. I was told it was easy to go overboard with such things, but that wouldn't happen if I didn't talk about them—or think about them.

After the army, I got a degree in religious studies, attended a seminary that specialized in Bible study, and two years later sailed for a tribal village in West Africa. As a missionary, I soon discovered that nothing in my church life, my education, or my theological studies—nothing—had prepared me for the war I was entering.

I didn't know it, but I was not entering the war for the first time by becoming a missionary. The war had always been all around me! It was just that now I was in a place where Satan's control had never been seriously challenged. I could more easily see the battle. These armies were spiritual rather than physical, but the casualties were just as real. Only years later did I understand that I had entered an active combat zone—as a reluctant warrior.

Oh, I knew Ephesians 6:12: The struggle was "not against flesh and blood, but against the rulers, against the authorities, against the powers of this dark world and against the spiritual forces of evil in the heavenly realms." I believed it—or I could quote the words. But that truth was only in my *brain*, not in my *heart*.

My own life proves that people can complete Bible college and theological seminary yet still file truth away in their brains without it affecting the control center of the heart. For us humans, the chasm between profession and practice (what we *say* we believe versus what we *do*) can be wide and deep!

Untwisting Truth

Besides not putting our knowledge into practice is the fact that we may have improperly learned key truths or had those truths twisted in some way. I certainly had not been led into a correct understanding of either my identity in Christ or my relationship as a believer to Satan and demons.

Satan creates evil by *perverting* what God created to be *good*. So one of Satan's favorite tactics is to cause us to view good and evil as extremes—answers are always easier at the extremes. On the subject of demons, the extremes are that demons are behind everything or behind nothing. If demons are not functional parts of our world, then we don't even have to think about them. And if they are behind all our problems, then we simply need to get rid of them. But if the truth is somewhere between those extremes, we need discernment, which involves more knowledge and responsibility than does taking the easy answers at the extremes.

Simon Peter helps us with this. His letters show us an older and wiser man than the Peter in the Gospels. He has learned many things, and he shares some of that learning with his readers. After reviewing some basics of the gospel, he commands, "Prepare your minds for action; be self-controlled" (1 Peter 1:13 NIV1984). He has learned that the spiritual battle is a battle for the mind. At the end of the letter, he comes back to that same theme:

> Be self-controlled and alert. Your enemy the devil prowls around like a roaring lion looking for someone to devour. Resist him, standing firm in the faith, because you know that your brothers throughout the world are undergoing the same kind of sufferings.
>
> 1 Peter 5:8–9 NIV1984

I am not sure how the idea of *resisting* got changed to *ignoring*. Certainly, if Satan cannot do anything to "good Christians," as some teach, Peter would have said, "Don't worry about the enemy. He can't touch you if you are a real believer."

But Peter's words under the guidance of the Holy Spirit are a powerful command to be "self-controlled and alert" in relation to this enemy. *Self-controlled* is the same word in 1 Peter 1:13 as in 1 Peter 4:7 about being ready for "the end of all things." Peter now tells us that we need to have the same attitude toward the devil, who is the "ruler" of this world. Peter is saying that we need to be *self-controlled and alert* because (as John says) "the whole world lies in the power of the evil one" (1 John 5:19 NASB).

Martin Luther had the right perspective when he wrote in his famous hymn, "And though this world with devils filled should threaten to undo us, we will not fear, for God has willed his truth to triumph through us." To be *alert* to the activity of the enemy is not to be demon-centered. We are to be *Christ*-centered and firm in our faith. Our lives are to be characterized by the confidence that in Christ we are more than conquerors (see Romans 8:37). But this does not mean that we ignore a desperate enemy committed to destroying our witness and ministry.

Peter knew something about the enemy's tactics from his early experience as a disciple—after all, Jesus said to him, "Get behind me, Satan!" (Matthew 16:23). Satan had been putting thoughts into Peter's mind without Peter realizing it. But Jesus was alert to the way Satan operates. He recognized the source of the thoughts. Peter didn't. He had not yet learned to be self-controlled and alert. Peter had declared, "Even if all fall away on account of you, I never will" (Matthew 26:33). When Jesus predicted that Peter would deny Him, Peter confidently affirmed, "Even if I have to die with you, I will never disown you" (verse 35).

Yet Peter's fear caused him *not* to be self-controlled and alert when the time came and he was confronted about his relationship to Jesus. He denied that he was a follower of Jesus and "began to call down curses, and he swore to them, 'I don't know the man!'" (Matthew 26:74). From his older and wiser perspective writing the epistles, Peter now speaks words of wisdom to all of us, in effect, "Be self-controlled and alert, because you have an enemy that is out to destroy you."

It is insanity to be in a war zone if you are not prepared to meet the enemy! But many Christians approach their spiritual enemy like this. Then they wonder why "bad things happen" to them. The problem is complicated, because the enemy is not visible to the eyes. Although camouflage can make a physical enemy hard to see, an invisible spiritual enemy increases the need for self-control and alertness.

It is so easy to see only the human side of life. We tend to forget that "what is seen is temporary, but what is unseen is eternal" (2 Corinthians 4:18). One of Satan's strategies is to get us to think and live within the limits of our time-space world. He has obviously been very successful with that strategy. Our culture conditions us to think this way. That kind of thinking makes it easy to believe that we should ignore the devil, not resist him.

Western culture's "Enlightenment worldview" has largely eliminated God and eternal truth from their central place. Paul warned, "See to it that no one takes you captive through hollow and deceptive philosophy, which depends on human tradition and the elemental spiritual forces of this world rather than on Christ" (Colossians 2:8). Clearly, Peter's command is still valid, even in this "enlightened" age. We need to be self-controlled and alert when it comes to all things spiritual, and that includes our spiritual enemy, the devil.

Notice also that Peter says, "the family of believers throughout the world is undergoing the same kind of sufferings" at the hands of this enemy (1 Peter 5:9). Satan and his demons are active in preliterate, tribal societies and sophisticated, enlightened Western ones. Satan's tactics may change, but his commitment to destroying the work of God hasn't diminished. Jesus said that this enemy comes to steal, kill, and destroy (see John 10:10), and he does not limit that activity to any geographic location.

So, although we may not *see* Satan and his demons, neither do we assume that we can just ignore them. These biblical warnings about Satan and demons are all addressed to believers; our basic attitude must therefore be one of self-control and alertness. We need spiritual discernment to perceive when we are dealing with this crafty enemy.

But how can an "ordinary" Christian get that kind of discernment? Jesus had a straightforward answer: He said that His sheep know the Shepherd's voice, "But they will never follow a stranger; in fact, they will run away from him because they do not recognize a stranger's voice" (John 10:5). Knowing the Shepherd's voice is not a matter of formal education; it comes by spending lots of time with Him, listening to Him so often that His voice and His truth are familiar. Then we begin to screen out any voice we don't recognize, because we *know* the familiar voice of our Shepherd. Discernment grows in relation to intimacy with our Shepherd.

The idea behind the term *self-control* is relevant here. The Greek word is translated "sober" in the King James Bible, and can mean "not intoxicated with wine or strong drink." But in the New Testament, it is almost always used as "not intoxicated with ideas and things of the world." A self-controlled person has heeded Paul's admonition to "stop being conformed to this world, but be transformed by the renewing of your mind" (Romans 12:2, author's translation). As the Phillips version reads, "Don't let the world around you squeeze you into its own mould, but let God re-mould your minds from within." A self-controlled person is one whose thinking is being reshaped by God's truth, not by the culture.

Self-controlled persons learn to ask the right questions based on their relationship with God and on their knowledge of what He has said is true. This means that they do not live in fear of our spiritual enemy, for Scripture is clear that he has been defeated by Christ through His cross and resurrection. Victory is available to us as God's children. But such persons will not just ignore this enemy, either. They will "resist him, standing firm in the faith" (1 Peter 5:9)—the faith that in Christ we are "more than conquerors" (Romans 8:37).

The Bible itself holds no long passages on demonology—because Jesus Christ is the focus of Scripture. If we therefore focus on knowing God and His ways, then we can begin to detect the deceptions of the father of lies. God didn't reveal Satan's ways or assignments in detail, because they change. Just as federal agents don't study counterfeit money, but the real thing, so they can detect the counterfeit, they also learn how counterfeiters work. In the same way, the Scriptures do not give us an "org chart" of the satanic realm. But they do affirm the reality of this enemy and provide the instruction we need to live in victory over him. Satan and demons were very evident in the days of Jesus' ministry, and He certainly didn't ignore this enemy. Neither should we.

We are never told that we will not have to fight. On the contrary, we are assured that we will. That is why we need to be *self-controlled and alert* and ready to resist, *standing firm in the faith* (see again 1 Peter 4:7; 5:8–9). We cannot exercise faith in what we do not know or really believe.

We do not fight in this war to determine who will win. That was settled once and for all at Jesus' crucifixion and resurrection (see Colossians 2:15; Hebrews 2:14–15). But we

are called on to *appropriate* that victory—to make it ours—
and to use the resources provided for us by the Captain of
our salvation until He calls us home or until the enemy is
finally consigned to his final destiny—the lake of fire.

What Am I Afraid Of?

If Christ has really conquered Satan and we participate in
that victory, why do we recoil in fear when it comes to Satan
and demons? Some try to deny that the battle exists. Others suppose that only a few are called to resist the enemy
and that they are given a special gift to do so. But Scripture
doesn't speak of any such gift. All Christians are to wear the
armor and use the weapons of this warfare. All Christians
are to submit to God and resist the enemy!

It's that old problem: We know truth in our heads, but it
doesn't get to our hearts, from which come the issues of life
(see Proverbs 4:23). This was evident in the life of Israel in
the Old Testament. God said through the prophet, "These
people come near to me with their mouth and honor me
with their lips, but *their hearts* are far from me" (Isaiah
29:13, emphasis added). Jesus said of the religious leaders
of His day who could quote the law and the prophets that
they were like tombs that looked good on the outside, but
inside were full of dead bones (see Matthew 23:27). Jesus
insisted, "By their fruit you will recognize them" (Matthew
7:16). Paul put it very clearly: "The kingdom of God is not
in words, but in power" (1 Corinthians 4:20 NASB).

Satan delights when Christians say by their *actions* that
they are afraid of him. Satan should run from the Christian,
not the Christian from Satan! Unfortunately, he uses fear—
of himself or of man (see Proverbs 29:25)—to stop many
soldiers. But the *fear of God* is the beginning of wisdom (see

Proverbs 9:10), not the fear of the devil or of what men will say. When we make the fear of God (that is, an awe, respect, and honor of Him) our focus, we can trust Him to take care of us. We don't need to fear anyone else.

A man came for counsel and said that while he was studying to be a missionary, his children began having nighttime disturbances. He understood that this was demonic and assumed that the attacks were related to his commitment to missionary service. He said, "I don't want my children going through this, so I'm getting out." He gave up his call to ministry.

My response was, "You think you have put your children in a safe place, but you have probably put them in the most dangerous place in the world. You have told Satan, 'I don't know a power stronger than yours. So, if you leave my children alone, I will leave you alone.'"

Satan will shake hands on an agreement like that! He loves to hear Christians express that kind of fear. The problem with such a deal is that Satan is a *liar*. He has no intention of living up to his end of such a bargain.

Fear of anything or anyone other than God is inconsistent with a genuine faith in God. Yes, fear is a normal first response. But as believers, we choose not to let fear control us. We choose to act in faith on the victory that has been won for us at the cross. "For God did not give us a spirit of timidity, but a spirit of power, of love and of self-discipline" (2 Timothy 1:7 niv1984).

Courage is not the absence of fear. Courage is action *in the presence of fear*. There is no need for courage if there is no fear involved. That's why Satan is the source of *dis*couragement. He does not want us to act with courage, so he *dis*courages us. God is the Encourager. He wants us to act with courage, so He *en*courages us. God has provided the basis on which we can act with courage. It is not just a matter of "whistling in the dark." It is a decision to act based on who God is and what He has done, rather than on a human perspective on the circumstances.

So even we authors are still reluctant warriors in one sense—we don't enjoy being involved in a battle, even though we are assured of victory. But, as we learned about spiritual warfare, we began to teach our students who were preparing for pastoral or missionary service how to fight. One reward of that teaching has been to meet graduates all over the world who have told us that our teaching on this subject was some of the most important learning they did.

But every believer will face the same spiritual enemy. Not only ministers and missionaries need to know how to fight. Let's not allow Satan to intimidate us and cause us to run away. Until Christ returns, the battle will go on, but we are more than conquerors through Him who loved us (see Romans 8:37). Let's live in that victory—not just in our heads, but in our hearts!

TWO

Know Your Identity

t's important to know your enemy. It's powerful to understand what strategies to use against him. But if you don't
know who *you* are, you're not ready to stand strong and
face his schemes. Part of this "boot camp" training is to help
you know who you are. Your identity is a powerful part of
dealing with the enemy.

When a new recruit shows up for military service, he or
she is given a uniform. Why? There was nothing wrong with
the clothing the recruits wore before—but now it's clear they
represent something larger than themselves. It's a matter of
identity. Drill sergeants "break you down to build you up"—
that is, they try to either give you an identity or strengthen
the one you already have. Identity is that important.

So, who do you think has a right to tell you who you are?
How do you know what to believe about yourself? And what
does God say about your identity?

How we answer these questions determines how we will
live, because we may not *live what we profess*, but we will

always *live what we believe.* We won't consistently act in any way that's inconsistent with what we believe about ourselves. God is the only source of truth, and the good news is, this includes the truth about who we are. We need to agree with God about ourselves, as well as about everything else in life.

Self-Identity

Books and articles abound on subjects like self-acceptance, self-image, and self-concept. Some say that the commandment to "love your neighbor as yourself" (Matthew 22:39) implies that we must love ourselves first before we can love others as we love ourselves. What about loving or not loving myself?

Let's define the word *self.* It's used several ways in Scripture. Now, no Greek word in the New Testament has an exact correspondence with our English word. English translations use *self* with several different meanings. We sometimes use the term *self* in self-denial—denying ourselves legitimate things in order to pursue higher things. But Jesus said, "If anyone wants to come after Me, *he must deny himself,* take up his cross, and follow Me" (Mark 8:34 NASB, emphasis added). The use of the term *self* in this implied command is the meaning Jesus had in mind when He said to the religious leaders of His day, "Woe to you, teachers of the law and Pharisees, you hypocrites! You clean the outside of the cup and dish, but inside they are full of greed and *self-indulgence*" (Matthew 23:25, emphasis added).

In Romans 2:8 Paul speaks of "those who are self-seeking and who reject the truth and follow evil." This is the self that is to be denied, or, as Paul puts it in Ephesians and Colossians, the self that is to be "put off" or "taken off" (Ephesians 4:22; Colossians 3:9). This self is my self-centered identity, rather than God-centered. It is evaluating ourselves using *our own criteria* rather than telling ourselves what God says about us. It is attempting to be *self*-sufficient instead of sufficient in Christ. Paul wrote, "Not that we are adequate in ourselves so as to consider anything as coming from ourselves, but our adequacy is from God" (2 Corinthians 3:5 NASB).

But two other uses of *self* are very different. One positive use refers simply to who I am as a person—the combination of physical and personality features that make up *me*. Many people express (verbally or by their actions) that they think God didn't do a very good job when He made them. They want different facial features, different talents, on and on. But the person God made each of us is to be accepted as God's handiwork. Paul says we are His *poema*, His artistic expression (see Ephesians 2:10). God's art is worthy to be loved—that's you!

The second positive use of self is what Paul means when he says we are to "put on the new self, created to be like God in true righteousness and holiness" (Ephesians 4:24, emphasis added). It is the new person each of us becomes by the grace of God. Paul told the Corinthians, "If anyone is in Christ, he is a new creation" (2 Corinthians 5:17 NKJV). This new creation is the Christ-centered, Spirit-filled child of God. This new creation is to be accepted as we agree with God's perception of who we are. It is the self in these last two senses that we love.

But *love* creates the same old problem: Words mean different things! The Greek language has at least four separate words for love. Three relate to an emotional response to the loved object or person. *Eros* is the Greek word for sensual or erotic love. It is usually self-gratifying (and so, ultimately *self*-loving). *Storge* is parental love; parents love their own offspring. Even *philia*, friendship or brotherly love, is limited to those with whom one shares common interests, goals, or relationships. These three types of love are found in every culture.

Agape is another kind of love, however. The Greeks didn't speak of this type often, because they thought it was a quality of the gods, not a human quality. And they were right, because "God is love" (1 John 4:16). God loves us because it is His *nature* to love us. That's why His love is unconditional—it doesn't depend upon the one to be loved, but upon the *nature of the lover*. Since we have become partakers of His divine nature (see 2 Peter 1:4), we can be like Christ and love others because of *who we are*, not because of *who they are* or what they can do for us. Jesus contrasts His love with human love in Luke 6:32: "If you love those who love you, what credit is that to you? Even sinners love those who love them."

This *agape* is the love we mean when we speak of loving ourselves. It's not self-centered, asking, *What do I think about myself?* Rather, it asks, *What does God say about me based on what He has already done for me?* Then we say, "I choose to agree with God." So I can thank God that He made me the way He did—including my body, my mind, and my talents. I accept His good work and agree with His purposes for me.

Are we supposed to love ourselves? Yes and no. It depends on what you mean by *self* and what you mean by *love*.

The Foundation of Me

If we are going to base our belief about and attitude toward ourselves on what God says about us, then we need to be

20

sure we know what God says. Satan surely doesn't want us to know and believe the truth. He knows that when we appropriate God's gracious and good work in us, our ability to live to God's glory explodes!

The battle for the mind begins right here in the life of a believer. Let's look at the figure below. It represents the relationship of the believer to God. There are two lines

Believer's Relationship to God

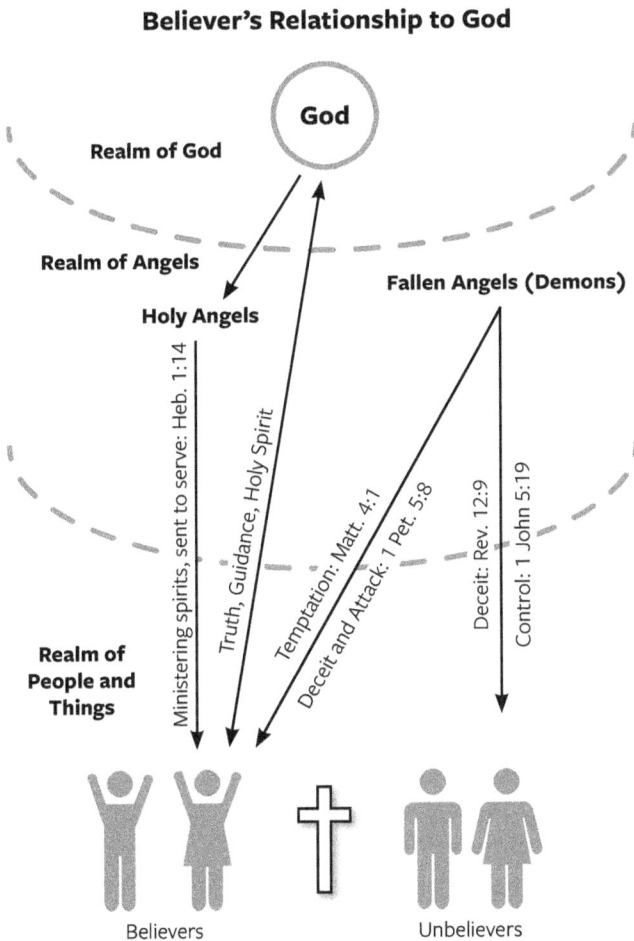

God

Realm of God

Realm of Angels

Holy Angels

Fallen Angels (Demons)

Ministering spirits, sent to serve: Heb. 1:14

Truth, Guidance, Holy Spirit

Temptation: Matt. 4:1

Deceit and Attack: 1 Pet. 5:8

Deceit: Rev. 12:9

Control: 1 John 5:19

Realm of People and Things

Believers

Unbelievers

between God and us. One line goes through the angels (the holy ones—those angels who did not follow Satan's rebellion). Notice that there is an arrow only at the bottom of the line, indicating that this is a one-way connection. We at no time approach God through angels. They are God's "ministering spirits sent to serve those who will inherit salvation" (Hebrews 1:14). They serve God by carrying out His orders, but they are in no sense mediators between God and us.

The other line, the one between God and us, has arrows at both ends, indicating that this is a two-way relationship. God talks to us; we talk to God. We have fellowship with Him in our love relationship with Him (see 1 John 1:3; Matthew 22:37; John 15:9).

There are two basic ideas here that are foundational: First, our relationship with God must be based on the *Holy Spirit's instruction, guidance, and empowerment*. Second, it must be based on *truth*. Experience teaches us that if we ignore these two foundations, we end up in trouble.

The Real Holy Spirit

When we talk about the Holy Spirit, we need to remember that our Western worldview conditions us to think that spirits don't have much to do with our daily lives. We are encouraged to act "on our own," based more on "reason and science" than on spiritual relationships. (However, this is leaning on our own understanding, exactly what Proverbs 3:5–6 tells us *not* to do!)

Still, we don't see spirits as very real. If you don't believe this, imagine that a discussion has heated up to where it's about to escalate into an argument. What motivates you to control those emotions? Your pastor showing up at the door, or the Holy Spirit, who is there with you? "But," you say, "that's not fair! You can see a person, but not the Holy Spirit."

That's just the point. We're conditioned to regulate our lives based more on the *people* we can see than on the Holy Spirit, who is present! We are taught to use "common sense" instead of God's revealed truth. Our culture squeezes us into its mold (see again Romans 12:2 PHILLIPS) more than we care to admit. Paul tells us that "what is seen is temporary, but what is unseen is eternal" (2 Corinthians 4:18). Too often, the temporary controls us, not the eternal. Worldliness is conforming to our culture's expectations, not to God's expectations.

But the real test of what we believe is our *actions*, not what we *say* we believe. The reason that there is often such a gap between what we *know* and what we *do* is that the Holy Spirit is not allowed to operate freely in our lives. When the Holy Spirit teaches us truth, it's life-changing! We can, however, "grieve the Holy Spirit" (Ephesians 4:30) by actions and words that are contrary to the fruit of love that is the hallmark of His presence in us (see Galatians 5:22). The Holy Spirit empowers us to know, and then to live out, the truth in our daily walk. When our relationship with Him is not flourishing, we may feel powerless against our enemy. Only Spirit-taught truth sets us free and enables us to resist the deceptions of our enemy.

Our perception that the spirit world is unreal carries over to the evil spirits in the supernatural, as well. We may have a theological knowledge about Satan and demons, but that knowledge does not often lead us to a functional faith in relating to them. "Demons" are often dealt with through prescribing powerful drugs or human reasoning, not through the Holy Spirit's power.

Truth and the Enemy

Admittedly, we can go too far in seeing demons behind every human problem. We can ascribe to them more power and influence than they have. Yet we can also go to the other extreme and not see them anywhere or anytime! We are not speaking here against the proper use of medications or reason, but we are warning against ignoring the role of evil spirits in our daily living—the principalities and powers against which Paul says we "struggle" (Ephesians 6:12). If Paul struggled with them, then the New Testament's warnings about this enemy need to be taken seriously.

In this God-created and God-sustained world, if we do things God's way, God will be responsible for the results. If we do things our way, we are held responsible for the results. Too many times, we do things our way and then want to blame God for the results. Too often, we practice what some call "selective obedience." We have our list of spiritual truths that we obey, but other truths outside our comfort zone that we do not obey. We act as if those things don't exist or don't apply to us.

We need to have a commitment to saying what God says about everything in our lives. You can be sure that Satan will take every opportunity possible to encourage us to have wrong responses to things that trouble us. He, in fact, is a master at suggesting a wrong response. This is all part of spiritual warfare.

Since Satan's primary tactic is deception, truth is an indispensable resource in resisting his attacks. Commitment to truth begins with truth revealed to us in the Word of God. The Word is the final authority for us in every area of life where it speaks.

Another aspect of truth that's also critically important is plain honesty—saying the truth about what's going on in our lives. Sadly, we humans are masters at pretending, especially in church. But church ought to be a place where it's safe to be honest, a place where you can go to find help with the things that are really troubling you. Often, instead of finding safety in church, we only find other hurting people. They don't know what to do for us, so they talk to others about us, avoid us, or just try to act as if there were no problem.

God meets us only at the point of our honesty. He cannot talk to a false self, only our true self. In effect, He says, *When you are ready to be honest about what is going on inside, I will be there to help you. But I cannot really help you until you can tell the truth—about yourself, and about Me.*

You cannot be right with God and not be honest with Him. God will put you through humbling experiences, if need be, so that you can be honest and able to be right with Him.

As the deceiver, Satan encourages us to wear a "false face." He wears his own mask most of the time, appearing as an "angel of light" or a "minister of righteousness" (see 2 Corinthians 11:13–15 NKJV). He encourages mask-wearing in those he influences. His purposes are well-served when "Christians" make a loud profession of faith while wearing their masks, but at the same time saying the opposite with the un-Christian way they handle some areas of their lives.

The technical term for this behavior is *hypocrisy*, and the Christian alternative to it is *sincerity*. Hypocrisy (Greek *hupokrites*, or "actor") is the idea of playing a part. In ancient times, actors used wax to create a new facial appearance. Sincerity, on the other hand, in the original language meant "without wax," without a false face. Sincere persons are just who they are. What you see is what you get. They are honest to the point of transparency, rather than seeking to hide the truth or even to deny what they know to be true. This is where truth transforms: "truth in the inward parts," which, according to David, is what God desires (Psalm 51:6 NKJV).

David had to learn this lesson the hard way. Psalm 32 is a song of David's experience with sin. When he tried to cover up his sin, it even affected his physical body (see verse 3). When he confessed, however—that is, when he spoke the truth, when he said about his sin what God said about it— he found forgiveness and could sing "songs of deliverance" (see verses 5, 7).

Sometimes our mask-wearing is not sin, but is a protective response to trauma or abuse. In this case, we need to acknowledge that the abuse we have suffered does not mean that *we* are bad, but that the *abuse* was wrong. Some people try to deal with their hurt by denying that it hurts. God can begin the healing process only when the hurt is acknowledged and grieved, and the offender is forgiven. "Blessed are those who mourn, for they will be comforted" (Matthew 5:4).

In being honest, we need to share our hurt and our sin with others (see James 5:16). God put us in the Body of Christ so that the Body could provide its strength to help us in the healing process, just as the healthy parts of our physical bodies provide strength for a hurting part. God intended the Church to be a place where it is safe to be honest—where you can go for help with the things that are really troubling you.

Hurting people often say, "There's no one I can talk to." What they mean is that there's no one they trust to handle the truth about them with love and with the hope of a solution. Often, someone who has been in counseling—even

Christian counseling—says, "I have never told this to anyone before, but . . ." People probably don't tell counselors everything because they are still not sure that a counselor really cares or *can* help them find resolution for their problems. The adage is, "People don't care how much you know until they know how much you care." Mature Christians should be available to help others know how much God cares, by the care we show.

Living free in Christ begins with a commitment to the truth—the truth about God, and the truth about what God says about us.

Let's Look Down

Yes, down. Did you know we are seated with Christ in the heavenly realms (see Ephesians 2:6)? This position, seated with Christ, is not just something we will attain in the future. Being "in Christ" is a present reality for the true believer.

Unfortunately, many of us live "under the circumstances" instead of "in Christ." We are never the helpless victims of our circumstances. We may very well create victimhood by the way we *look* at our circumstances, but in Christ we can always be "more than conquerors." Let's look at this idea of how we should see ourselves "in Christ."

Scripture uses many figures of speech to help us understand our relationship to God. One is "children by adoption."

Paul uses the idea of adoption in Ephesians 1:4–5: "In love he [God] predestined us for adoption to sonship through Jesus Christ, in accordance with his pleasure and will." Adoptions are very intentional. The adoptive parents *want* the child. They *choose* the child. Paul tells us that God chose to adopt us as His children, "in accordance with his *pleasure and will*" (emphasis added).

God does not adopt us *out of* our earthly families, but adoption into His family may affect the way we relate to our earthly families. We no longer need to see ourselves as the victims of the way we were treated by our parents or families, because God has now made us part of His family—a family where our perfect Father loves with unconditional love. He can be depended upon to use His limitless power to do what His love chooses is best for us.

Who Told You Who You Are?

Most of us have received messages from others that tell us who we are. Quite often, those messages come to us so early in life that we don't question them. And the enemy loves the ones that are lies. For instance, if you grew up learning that you had to be almost perfect to be acceptable to God, the devil will use that lie to make you think you'll never be good enough for God to use. If you were told you're stupid, ugly, and clumsy, it's possible that you still hear that voice in your head. The enemy piles onto that lie, repeating it to us and telling us that we can never be good enough for God to use.

We live in a very performance-based society, meaning there are lies we all live under. We constantly compare ourselves with others, deeply concerned about what people think of us. When our behavior is determined by what other people say we are or by what we think they say we are, rather than by who we perceive ourselves to be "in Christ," we are headed back toward victimhood.

But here is the remedy for those lies: seeing ourselves from God's perspective—as who we are in Christ! The list of who I am "in Christ" could be much longer. But it's a start at looking at ourselves from God's perspective.

Myself Seen Through a Filter

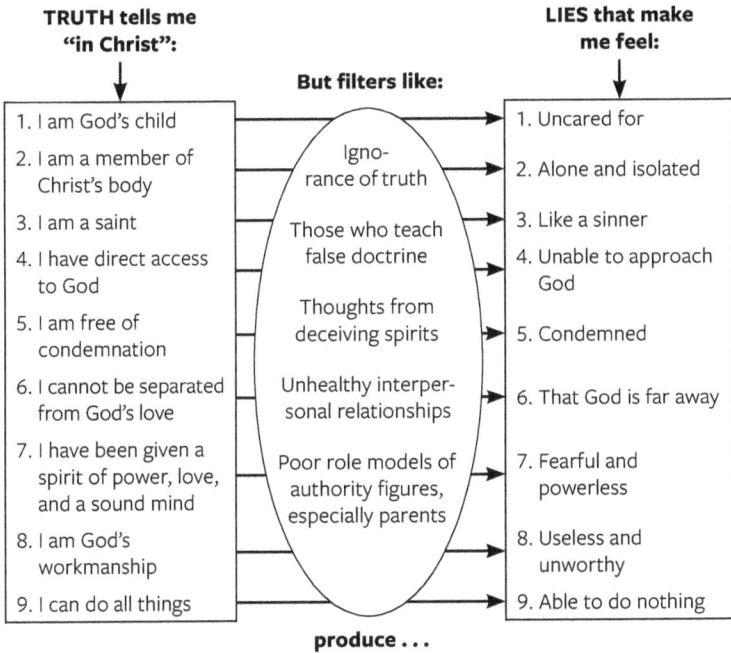

TRUTH tells me "in Christ":	But filters like:	LIES that make me feel:
1. I am God's child	Igno-rance of truth	1. Uncared for
2. I am a member of Christ's body		2. Alone and isolated
3. I am a saint	Those who teach false doctrine	3. Like a sinner
4. I have direct access to God		4. Unable to approach God
5. I am free of condemnation	Thoughts from deceiving spirits	5. Condemned
6. I cannot be separated from God's love	Unhealthy interpersonal relationships	6. That God is far away
7. I have been given a spirit of power, love, and a sound mind	Poor role models of authority figures, especially parents	7. Fearful and powerless
8. I am God's workmanship		8. Useless and unworthy
9. I can do all things		9. Able to do nothing

produce . . .

Since we were all born dead in our trespasses and sins (see Ephesians 2:1), we didn't have the presence of God or know His ways. So living under lies and false filters, we try to earn a sense of worth according to the world system in which we have been raised—based mainly on our appearance, performance, and status. But our attempts at self-verification always crumble.

Even when we do great things, they may not be affirmed by others. So we get discouraged, even though the lack of affirmation may be due to the other person's own problems or upbringing. We're born with only two fears: fear of loud noises, and fear of falling. Every other fear is *learned* somewhere—and those learned fears often drive us to behaviors and to thinking that leaves out who God says we are.

Shame is another common way that we all have been influenced. If it isn't people who provide the shame messages, it's Satan and his corps of demons. Satan is called "the accuser of our brothers and sisters" (Revelation 12:10), and he loves to accuse us of anything he can. Satan knows that if we already have a negative perception of ourselves, we will respond to his accusations by behaving in essentially negative ways. He scores, and we are confused: *Why did I do that? What just happened? Why am I so hurt?*

From there on, it doesn't matter what new truth we learn in our heads. Unless we apply the truth about our identity "in Christ" to ourselves daily, no amount of behavior modification is going to turn us into Spirit-led Christians. People will only behave in a way that's consistent with the way they see themselves.

Many Christians swing back and forth between trying hard and giving up—trying to do and say the things that will bring affirmation, but receiving enough shame that they feel like giving up. Imagine: Who would you be if you did not have shame, fear, or guilt?

Agreeing with God

We spoke earlier about loving ourselves by saying about ourselves what God says about us. Let's look at this in terms of adoption, which we also spoke about a little. Anyone who has adopted children can tell you that this process is intentional. In the process of adopting children, a judge will ask the prospective parents, "Do you understand that in adopting this child, you must make the child an heir with any other children born to your marriage?" Likewise in God's family, adopted children are equal heirs with God's Son, Jesus Himself! In Romans 8:16–17, Paul says, "The Spirit himself testifies with our spirit that we are God's children. Now if we are children, then we are heirs—heirs of God and co-heirs with Christ." With our background in receiving lies and false filters, it can be difficult to think of ourselves as royalty in God's Kingdom. "A prince or princess?" you ask. Yes, isn't that what a co-heir to the King would be? This is not prideful—you are believing truth!

Do you see why Satan doesn't want you to believe this? If you did, and you started to live like royal children in God's Kingdom, you would bring glory to God in a way impossible when you are dragging around as a victim, saying you're no good. You may upgrade the "no good" to "a sinner saved by grace." But as great as having our sins forgiven and being "saved" is, it's only half of the gospel. The other half is understanding and accepting the fact that *God has* "raised us up with Christ and seated us with him in the heavenly realms in Christ Jesus" (Ephesians 2:6). This is the judge pardoning the accused and then adopting him into his own family and making him his heir. What can we say except "Hallelujah!"?

The way we define our belief about who we are never depends ultimately on what others think. Paul said, "When they measure themselves by themselves and compare themselves with themselves, they are not wise" (2 Corinthians 10:12). We get our identity from an entirely new source, namely, who we are in Christ based on what God has already done for us. What we have done, good or bad, is not part of the equation. So we can rest—because our victory ultimately depends on *what God has already done*, not on what we try to do.

Here's a great historic illustration. J. Hudson Taylor was a young man with a vision to go into the interior of China. In the 1850s, no missionary had yet ventured there. To prepare, he adopted a very disciplined lifestyle. He ate a very Spartan diet, and he cut himself off from sources of money so that he could learn to trust God to supply his needs. (That's faith!)

He went to China as he planned. He wore Chinese clothing and let his hair grow so he could wear it in a long braid. He wanted to identify with the people he was trying to reach with the gospel. He eventually founded a new mission and asked God for one hundred missionaries and enough money in big gifts to send them out so that he wouldn't have a lot of bookkeeping. God answered his prayer!

But when Taylor went around to visit the missionaries, there was tension between them and this super-spiritual, super-disciplined leader. He finally realized that in spite of his big prayers being answered, he was guilty of unbelief. How could that be? He realized that he was trying hard *in his own efforts* to impress God and himself and everyone else with how committed he was. But God made it clear to Taylor that He wanted him to *rest* in what He had done. Hudson realized that he was simply *not believing* in and *receiving* the gracious gift Jesus offered.

From that time on, when Taylor visited the missionaries, blessing overflowed, not tension. When he exchanged his performance-based approach to Christianity for a *grace-based relationship* with his Savior, his behavior changed. Even missionaries may not live what they *say* they believe— but they will always *live* what they *really believe*!

Hudson Taylor's favorite song became the hymn "Jesus, I Am Resting, Resting" by Jean Sophia Piggot:

> Jesus, I am resting, resting,
> in the joy of what thou art.
> I am finding out the greatness

of thy loving heart.
Thou hast bid me gaze upon thee,
and thy beauty fills my soul;
For by thy transforming power,
thou hast made me whole.

In Romans 5:1–5, Paul has an interesting commentary on people living what they really believe. Let's quote from The Living Bible (emphasis added):

> So now, since we have been made right in God's sight by faith in his promises, we can have real peace with him *because of what Jesus Christ our Lord has done for us.* For because of our faith, he has brought us into this place of highest privilege where we now stand [seated with God in the heavenlies in Christ], and we confidently and joyfully look forward to actually becoming all that God has had in mind for us to be [as His adopted children].
>
> We can rejoice, too, when we run into problems and trials, for we know that they are good for us—they help us learn to be patient. And patience develops strength of character in us and helps us trust God more each time we use it until finally our hope and faith are strong and steady. Then, when that happens, we are able to hold our heads high no matter what happens and know that all is well, for we know how dearly God loves us, and we feel this warm love everywhere within us because God has given us the Holy Spirit to fill our hearts with his love.

Does holding our heads high no matter what happens sound like pride? It would be, if it were based on the "try hard–give up" cycle of performance-driven, fearful, false-self religion. But it isn't. It's based on what God has done for us in Christ. It's the result of *receiving* His gracious gift to us—adoption into His family. That might seem like we're not "doing" anything, and you're right! It was all done by Jesus when He said, "It is finished." All He asks us to do is to believe what He says and receive what He offers. Not believing this is not humility; it is *unbelief*, no matter what Satan tries to tell you to the contrary.

The feelings of inferiority most of us deal with are the result of asking self-centeredly *what we think about ourselves.* But true humility is not thinking "less of" ourselves, but thinking of ourselves less! It is confidence properly placed—in God, not in ourselves. Inferiority is Satan's counterfeit for humility.

We also need to recognize that the path to "strong and steady" hope and faith leads through learning to deal with "problems and trials." Most of us would like to avoid that part of the journey, but as a good and wise Father, God wants His children to develop "strength of character" that can come in no other way. How we handle the hard places in life will depend on whether we see ourselves as under the circumstances or far above them.

The figure below shows the believer seated "in Christ" in the heavenly realms. It is from this perspective that we look at ourselves and our circumstances. Things look very different from up there. Our prayers go to our Father, with whom we are sitting in a love relationship! The Bible is read with the Author at our side. Witnessing becomes simply living out our position as joint heirs with Christ—a position that makes us spiritual princes and princesses in His Kingdom. Resisting the devil also is very different from this perspective. If you see yourself as a victim, way down at the bottom, you will be very reluctant to stand against a powerful spiritual enemy so far above you. But seated with God in the heavenlies, with

Warfare Relationship

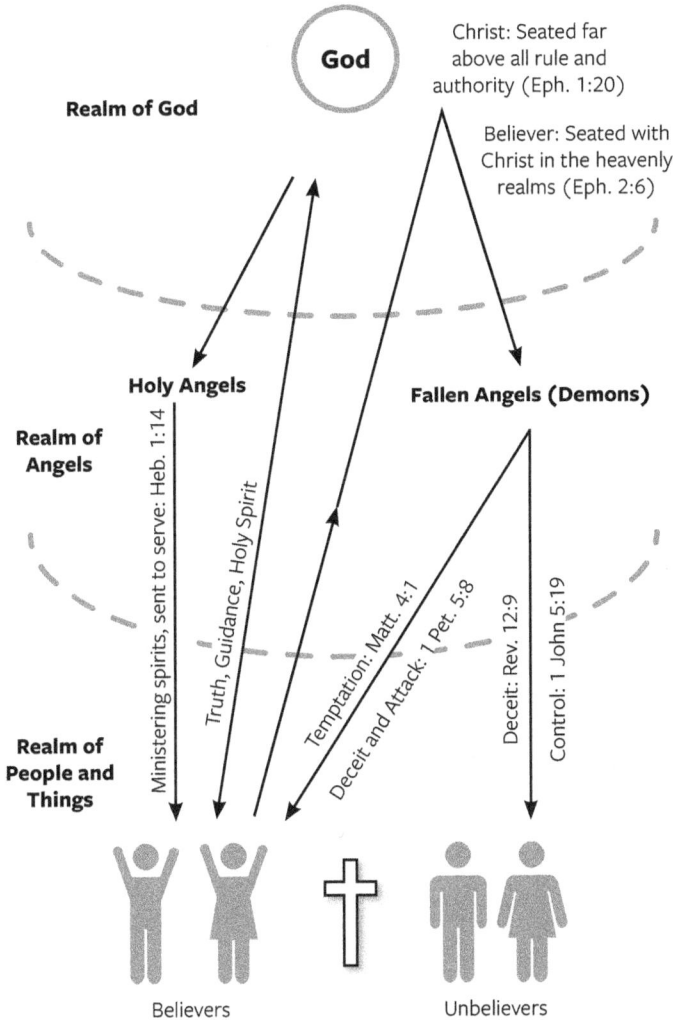

God

Christ: Seated far above all rule and authority (Eph. 1:20)

Realm of God

Believer: Seated with Christ in the heavenly realms (Eph. 2:6)

Holy Angels

Fallen Angels (Demons)

Realm of Angels

Ministering spirits, sent to serve: Heb. 1:14

Truth, Guidance, Holy Spirit

Temptation: Matt. 4:1

Deceit and Attack: 1 Pet. 5:8

Deceit: Rev. 12:9

Control: 1 John 5:19

Realm of People and Things

Believers

Unbelievers

your hand on the arm of the throne of God, you can resist the enemy "steadfast[ly] in the faith" (1 Peter 5:9 NKJV).

Now do you understand why we say, "Keep looking down"? It all depends on where you are looking down from. Being "in Christ" changes your perspective on prayer, witnessing, reading the Bible, resisting the enemy. It even changes your perspective on suffering. Paul says, "I consider that our present sufferings are not worth comparing with the glory that will be revealed in us" (Romans 8:18). Being a co-heir with Jesus means that there is glory waiting for us—glory that Satan will never get, glory that is our sure inheritance as children of God. Few of us have suffered as much as Paul did, so we need to listen to him when he tries to help us see things from our position "in Christ."

It's Who I Am

We began by asking, *Who are we? Who told us who we are?* We know Satan wants to give us all the *wrong* answers to these questions. God is the source of truth as we seek the right answer.

We need to speak the truth about who we are as God's redeemed children. But to speak the truth about anything, including what it means to be God's child in our true God-given identity, we need to be sure we are relating to God as *He* really is. We will look at that next.

THREE

Know Your King

W e're learning to agree with God about who we are. We're starting to recognize the lies of the enemy. Now, the battle for the mind begins! How we perceive *God* determines how we perceive almost everything else in life.

Satan knows this, and that's why he almost always begins his attacks on us by trying to give us a twisted view of God. This is important, because again, while we may not practice what we *say* we believe, we will always *practice* what we *really* believe. For this reason, we need to examine how we view God.

Nothing New Here

Let's look at how the serpent tempted Eve in the garden of Eden. The serpent (Satan) first tricked Eve into questioning whether God (and what He said) could be trusted. The serpent said to her,

Has God said that you will die if you eat of that tree? . . .
That's not true. You won't die. You will become like God
Himself, knowing good and evil. You won't have to take your
orders from Him anymore because your judgment is as good
or even better than His. You will be better off if you do what
you think is right than if you do what He says. You see, God
just cannot be trusted completely.

Genesis 3:1, 4–5, author's paraphrase

The serpent also implied that God did not really love
Adam and Eve, or He would not have withheld this wonderful fruit from them. The Scriptures tell us that the fruit was
"good for food and pleasing to the eye, and also desirable for
gaining wisdom" (Genesis 3:6). How could God really love
them and withhold this wonderful "blessing" from them?
Satan was clearly seeking to undermine God's character, and
once Adam and Eve began to doubt God's trustworthiness
and love, it was easy for the serpent to lead them to break
the one negative command God had given.

This is how human nature has worked ever since. It's like
a child with a roomful of toys, who says, "I have nothing!
You won't let me play with the *matches*!" We so often focus
on the one thing we know we shouldn't have. God had told
Adam and Eve that they could eat from *every other tree* in
the garden. It wasn't as if they didn't have wonderful fruit on
many other trees. All they had to do to remain in perfect fellowship with their Creator was to obey one command. They
could not have had it much easier. Yet once they doubted
whether God could be trusted, they now had to make all
their own decisions.

Think of what a score this was for the enemy, getting them
to believe that if God couldn't be trusted in *one* thing, He
couldn't be trusted in any. If their judgment was better than

God's in this matter, it might be better than God's in every other matter. That kind of responsibility was overwhelming—and it still is! Most of us live under the lie that "it's all on me" and "I have to do this myself."

Satan is a clever deceiver—what appeared to be only a matter of eating or not eating fruit from one tree had far bigger consequences than Adam and Eve ever dreamed. Before, they had had an open, trusting relationship with God. Now they hid from God—for reasons they didn't even understand, for they'd never known shame, guilt, or fear before. Their needs had all been met by God up to that point. Now that they had lost their trusting relationship with Him, however, they were about to lose the whole garden. Before they fell for Satan's lies, their relationship with their Creator had met their human need for significance. Now they had lost that relationship, and with it their significance as God's children.

Sin's consequences are always greater than what Satan mentions when he dangles the forbidden fruit in front of us. Even after a sin has been confessed and forgiven, consequences persist: Angry words can never be taken back; injury caused to another cannot be undone. And it all begins when we see God as someone other than who He really is.

Same Old Counterfeits

Since his first success in the garden of Eden, Satan has gone on to bigger and bigger lies about God. The first one is to convince some people that there is no such person as God and no supernatural power (see Psalm 53:1). "What you see here is all you get," he says. "There is no life beyond the grave."

Sometimes the counterfeit god Satan holds up is the universe itself. Everything and every person is said to be "part of god." One simply cannot separate the spiritual and the physical, because "they are all one." This is the belief system behind many practices originating in the East. New Age practitioners in the West take this view: They say our sin is in not recognizing that we are really god, or at least part of god, and that we can control our own destiny by exercising our goodness. We do not need a Savior to die for our sins. We can manipulate psychic power in the universe to make it do what we want. These animistic ideas are nothing new. They are as old as history. Instead of the biblically forbidden *medium*, the New Age renames such a person a *channeler*, and *demons* have been renamed *spirit guides*. (We'll talk more about animism in the next chapter; this is simply a variation on that.)

Some people add to their belief system all kinds of other gods who share all the worst qualities of fallen human beings, like the gods in the Greek and Roman cultures of biblical times. We call this polytheism. These pantheons of gods might have one high god above the others, but the role of the God of the Bible as Creator, Sustainer, and Savior had been lost.

Some come closer to the truth by seeing their god as the creator of the world, but he is very far away and virtually impossible to reach, unapproachable by mere humans. Relating to him is reduced to an endless repetition of memorized prayers and certain prescribed activities. Then all kinds of magic and sorcery are added. These are some of Satan's favorite ways to control people under his influence—along with fear, shame, and guilt in an endless cycle, with no forgiveness.

Religion or Relationship?

You may be saying, "Thank God *we* are not like that. We Bible believers know who God really is."

The problem is, as we have noted already, we may *know* *truth* in our heads, but that does not guarantee that we will *live* it. We may easily become practical atheists, knowing all about God, yet not *knowing* Him at all. We can *say* we know God, but do we *live* as though He doesn't exist? That's another false god, the Sunday-only God to whom we give our hour or two a week, and then we go our own way, doing it all ourselves!

But God wants to lead us into a personal relationship with Him—a love relationship! He is more than a God confined to the pages of theology books, or even to the Bible. We can easily become like the Pharisees, to whom Jesus said, "You study the Scriptures diligently because you think that in them you have eternal life. These are the very Scriptures that testify about me, yet you refuse to come to me to have life" (John 5:39–40). Satan does not object to orthodox theology—so long as it does not lead us to an intimate relationship with God.

Caricatures of God

Have you ever seen an artist doing caricatures? It's kind of scary to see the distortions—a big chin, unusual hairdo, pear-shaped body. You can tell who has been caricatured, but the drawing is not an accurate portrayal—that's the point!

Satan tries to do this with God. Because the Bible says God is our Judge, Satan emphasizes God's role as Judge out of all proportion to His role as loving Father or giver of good gifts. Some people feel condemned no matter what they read in the Bible, because they have agreed with the caricature of God as Judge, condemning them in every way short of perfection.

God Seen Through a Filter

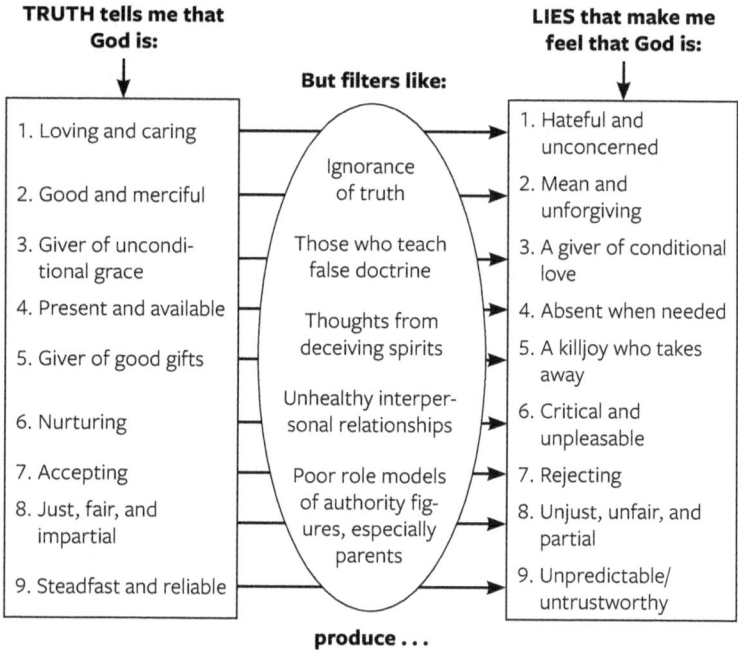

TRUTH tells me that God is:	But filters like:	LIES that make me feel that God is:
1. Loving and caring	Ignorance of truth	1. Hateful and unconcerned
2. Good and merciful		2. Mean and unforgiving
3. Giver of unconditional grace	Those who teach false doctrine	3. A giver of conditional love
4. Present and available	Thoughts from deceiving spirits	4. Absent when needed
5. Giver of good gifts		5. A killjoy who takes away
6. Nurturing	Unhealthy interpersonal relationships	6. Critical and unpleasant
7. Accepting	Poor role models of authority figures, especially parents	7. Rejecting
8. Just, fair, and impartial		8. Unjust, unfair, and partial
9. Steadfast and reliable		9. Unpredictable/ untrustworthy

produce ...

For others, God is another caricature—the kindly old grandfather who spoils His grandchildren. Far from correcting them, He may laugh at their sins. Either extreme pleases Satan equally well because such caricatures keep people from the truth.

A Filtered Image

When we take a photo, we often have a choice of filters—ways we can make the photo look different from the true original. Our view of God is also often changed and distorted from its true original through family or cultural filters that distort His image. Satan knows that our view of God often comes to us through other people. We believe what we receive, especially as young children. He will use this as a means of distorting the true image of God in our minds and hearts. The figure above suggests how this filtering process works.

This is what God said concerning Israel in Hosea's time: "My people are destroyed from lack of knowledge" (Hosea 4:6). This is true in any age. What we don't know *can* hurt us, especially when it comes to a correct view of God.

When we don't know the truth, we easily pick up deception from false teachers. Cults prey on people raised in Christian culture who have not come into a personal relationship with Jesus, or who have received the gospel but have not grown. Cults or cultlike expressions of the Church offer these people a form of discipleship, but these forms depend on following a self-appointed leader, based on a wrong view of God.

When Jesus had to tell Peter "Get behind Me, Satan" because of Peter's thoughts, we saw how Satan can put thoughts into our minds. This is what is behind Paul's statement to his "son in the faith," Timothy: "The Spirit clearly says that in later times some will abandon the faith and follow deceiving spirits and things taught by demons" (1 Timothy 4:1). This teaching of demons often comes through false teachers, but it may also come through thoughts that Satan or one of his fallen angels places directly in the mind of a person. This is a primary means of temptation, but in this case, it brings the person into bondage through wrong and even blasphemous views of God.

It's not unusual for people to report that they hear voices in their minds condemning them or suggesting blasphemous thoughts to them. Satan will try to get you to believe that these are *your own* thoughts, and if you fall for this, you will be in bondage to the lies you believe. The con artist uses this filter to skew our view of God. He knows how vulnerable we are to such deception. We need to know that our defense is to "take captive every thought to make it obedient to Christ" (2 Corinthians 10:5). This is another reason we need to remember our identity in Christ!

Dysfunctional relationships with other people, especially authority figures, are often the filter that distorts our view of God. These relationships may be with teachers, pastors, coaches, or anyone with whom we developed a close relationship. By far the most important persons in this category are parents. We very easily carry over our view of our human father to our heavenly Father. The parent for whom nothing we do is ever good enough may filter into our view of God— the God who is impossible to please. A painful relationship with an abusive parent filters our view of God into one who finds more pleasure in punishing us than in blessing us.

We have all been victimized in some way, but whether we *remain victims* is really our choice. Nobody can fix our past, and even God doesn't try to do that. Instead, He makes us a new creation in Christ and sets us free from our past. We choose to believe the truth that will set us free. The true knowledge of God and who we are as His children is what liberates us.

The Hard-to-Please God

Satan is clever enough to recognize that if he can get us to buy his wrong view of God, we will almost certainly have a wrong view of what it means to be God's child. Have you seen yourself looking at God through any of the filters mentioned here or shown in the figure about God seen through a

44

filter? Most people do at some point. But if you are feeling good about your view of God so far, let's look at one more very common filter in our thinking about God. Look at the following words:

Authority • Accountability • Affirmation • Acceptance

How do those words describe your relationship with God? Does He say, "Only as you are accountable to My authority will I affirm and accept you"? Or does He say, "I accept you and affirm you, and ask for accountability to My authority"?

An evangelical pastor who came for help with a problem was asked this question, and with no hesitation he said, "Oh, it is definitely in the order of accountability before acceptance. I have to conform to God's expectations of me if I expect Him to affirm me."

The answer to him was, "Do you know what you have just told me? You have said you believe that you can only earn the grace of God. I tell you that that is impossible! You can never get to acceptance and affirmation by God through the avenue of your behavior, because 'a person is not justified by the works of the law' (Galatians 2:16). That was true on the day you were saved and on every day after!"

The lie that God demands accountability from us without granting us acceptance and affirmation comes from our authority figure filter. When authority figures demand accountability without extending acceptance and affirmation, they will never get it. But when authority figures grant acceptance and affirmation, their subjects voluntarily become accountable—another reason for the enemy to make sure human authority figures distort our view of God. One of Satan's favorite lies about God is that we must be *good enough* to be loved and accepted by Him, and that God is hard to please.

God's standards are very high, Satan will tell you, and when you think you are making progress, you will discover that the goal has been moved. Most Christians know this is not true, but when we examine the way we *live*, our actions often deny our profession.

Our whole society is performance based. You earn your way up the corporate ladder, the social ladder, the academic ladder, the sports ladder, on and on. If we are bringing that kind of thinking into our relationship with God, we must shift our thinking! According to the Bible, we are acceptable to God based *only* on what God has done *for us in Christ*, not on what we do for Him.

We all long for acceptance and affirmation. But there are two wrong ways to look for acceptance. One is to continually take our own spiritual temperature to see if we are "good enough." When we do this, we become trapped in either pride or inadequacy. Only God can give us a right view of ourselves and fulfill our need for affirmation and acceptance.

When we look for acceptance from other people, peer pressure tends to control our lives. We "keep up" with the neighbors and focus on our appearance and performance. We strive for mastery to receive the praise of people. If our functional faith is filtering out the true God who is unconditionally loving and abounding in grace—qualities that result in acceptance and affirmation—we will turn to people for the acceptance and affirmation we need.

Everyone needs to be loved. But no human is capable of giving unconditional love and acceptance. It first comes from God, who loves because *it is His nature* to love (see 1 John 4:8). As humans, we tend to love people who are lovable. Then we tend to expect God to love only what *we consider lovable*. Our tendency to create God in our own image, or in the image of significant others, is another one of the devil's favorite filtering strategies he uses to trap us.

We also need to begin with a God who expresses His love in grace. To understand the grace of God, we need to understand that *justice* is getting what we deserve. A man accused of a crime stands before the judge, who says, "You're guilty. The penalty is death." God does not deal with us on the basis of justice.

Mercy means *not* getting what you deserve. The accused stands before the judge, who says, "You're guilty, but I am dismissing the sentence. You are free." But God cannot be unjust. So the penalty for sin had to be paid, and Jesus did that at the cross: "God made him who had no sin to be sin for us, so that in him we might become the righteousness of God" (2 Corinthians 5:21). Justice and mercy meet at the cross. Paul wrote to Titus, "When the kindness and love of God our Savior appeared, he saved us, not because of righteous things we had done, but *because of his mercy*" (Titus 3:4–5, emphasis added).

God's mercy, which offers us forgiveness and freedom from the penalty for sin, is indeed great good news. But it's only the beginning! There is *grace*. Grace is getting what you could *never* deserve. The accused stands before the judge, who says, "You're guilty, but I'm waiving the sentence, and I'm going to adopt you and make you my heir." Paul tells us that "the Spirit himself testifies with our spirit that we are God's children. Now if we are children, then we are heirs—heirs of God and co-heirs with Christ" (Romans 8:16–17).

Which God?

So which God do you worship? The one who has been distorted by the filters of the world or twisted by the enemy of our souls? Is He a hard-to-please God who keeps moving the standard just a little higher? Or is He the utterly trustworthy God whose Word is forever settled in heaven (see Psalm 119:89)? Is He the God who loves you with unconditional love—love that does not depend on how lovable you are, but on *His very nature as love*? Is He the God of the Bible? Or an idol of your own making? Do you really know Him? Or is He a caricature—a cartoon figure—that you carry in your mind?

To win the spiritual battle for our minds, we must have a true view of God. That's why Paul prayed for the Ephesians "that the God of our Lord Jesus Christ, the Father of glory, may give you a spirit of wisdom and of revelation in the knowledge of Him" (Ephesians 1:17 NASB). This could be translated as "full knowledge" or "right knowledge." It is as if Paul is saying, "I know Satan will be trying to pervert your view of God, so I want to begin by making sure that you know who God really is." This is where we all need to begin our spiritual journey!

FOUR

Know Your Worldview

Everyone lives by faith—all of the time! The only difference between Christian and non-Christian faith is the *object* of our faith. Christians believe God and His Word. Before we came to Christ, however, we believed in something or someone else. Even if we have been Christians since childhood, we have developed certain attitudes and beliefs about ourselves and the world in which we live—our worldview. We talked about filters that distort our view of God in the previous chapter. Now let's talk about the views of the world that we have accepted.

Our worldview is something else we received without knowing it was happening. Assumptions about who we are, who others are, and how the world works—and who God is and how He works—were all laid down in us long before we could think about such things! These views are the set of filters through which we pass all input from the world around us, to give it meaning.

Most of us are not even conscious of having a worldview. We absorbed it from the culture in which we were reared. It never dawned on us that we should question it. We make significant judgments about the events in our lives—judgments that may very well be based on faulty worldviews, according to Scripture. A quick way to discover your own worldview is to move to a place where the worldview is very different from the one with which you grew up.

When I (Tim) went to West Africa as a missionary, my wife and I served in a typical tribal village. The people were animists with a strong belief in the spirit world. People sometimes say, "I suppose you saw a lot of spiritual warfare out there."

My response is, "No, I didn't. I wouldn't have recognized it if I had seen it." I had degrees from a Christian college, a theological seminary, and a major American university. But nowhere did anyone help me understand what my own worldview was or anything about the worldview of the people to whom I was to minister, especially their beliefs about the spirit world.

So when I heard the Africans talk about spirit activity, I filtered it as "superstition." That's why I didn't see a lot of spiritual warfare—not because it wasn't there, but because my worldview kept me from recognizing it. Beyond things that the Africans said and did, as Westerners we tended to see even the things other missionaries said and did as problems with only human dimensions. Spiritual warfare was almost *never* seen as a possible element in the relationships between missionaries, even when those relationships were fraught with problems!

In our Western worldview, we tend to ignore Satan and demons, although the Bible never tells us to ignore the devil.

On the contrary, the Bible tells us to *resist* the devil. The Greek word translated "resist" or "stand against" is the same in Ephesians 6:13, James 4:7, and 1 Peter 5:9. Even the apostle Paul had "a messenger of Satan, to torment" him (2 Corinthians 12:7), and Satan "hindered" him from carrying out his plans to visit Thessalonica (1 Thessalonians 2:18 KJV).

If our worldview is a filter not solidly based on biblical teaching, we will arrive at faulty or dangerous conclusions about our experiences. We must conclude that often, our Western worldview filters are faulty. Yet our worldview is critically important! The most logical reason that the Church has never dealt with all this is that Satan has been successful in his deception, getting us to think that all is well with our worldview.

This is what Paul had in mind when he wrote to the Romans, "Stop being conformed to this world" (Romans 12:2, author's translation). Being conformed or not conformed to this world goes back to the way we see and interpret what we experience. Worldview also underlies Jesus' statement, "You will know the truth, and the truth will set you free" (John 8:32).

Three Worldviews

If we take a closer look at three basic worldviews, it may help us understand what we are talking about. We seldom find a society where all the people hold the exact same worldview, but understanding some differences in three worldviews—animism, a Western outlook, and the biblical worldview—will help us see how our beliefs are shaped by these filters.

Animism: A World Controlled by Spirits

Animism is the belief that spiritual power and spirit beings have a role in almost everything that happens. It's found in most tribal societies of our world, but many elements of it are also found in most modern societies. Animism is concerned mainly with the practical realities of daily life. Let's look at some general common beliefs associated with this worldview.

Most animists believe in a creator or main god of some kind, but they mainly see him as far removed from them. Contact is unlikely, if not impossible. Therefore, our figure shows a "God" in parentheses far up at the top. While this god may be referred to in rituals, he does not play a very significant role in daily life.

The sources of spiritual power in the animists' approach to daily life are (1) an impersonal spiritual power (called

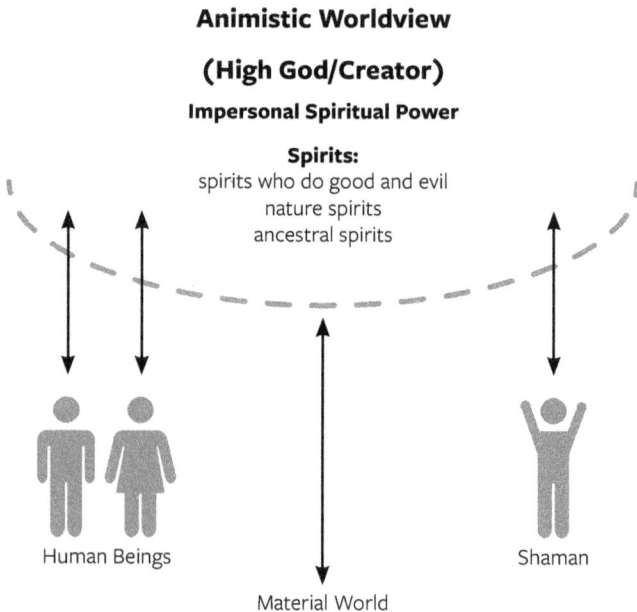

Animistic Worldview

(High God/Creator)

Impersonal Spiritual Power

Spirits:
spirits who do good and evil
nature spirits
ancestral spirits

Human Beings

Shaman

Material World

mana by anthropologists) that is thought to permeate everything in the universe, and (2) spirits of many types.

Especially in Asia, the impersonal spiritual power may be called *god*. This, in turn, may lead to the belief that everyone and everything is part of this impersonal god. But more often, it is thought to be a power much like electricity, neither good nor evil. Whether it produces good or evil depends on how human beings relate to it. Just as electricity can be generated and channeled, *mana* is thought to be controlled. (You may remember similar New Age teachings—truly, not much has changed!)

And just as we have specialists in dealing with electricity (because handled improperly, it can kill you), so animists use a specialist, a spiritual electrician, so to speak, to handle problems facing them in the spirit realm. This person is called a shaman, a witch doctor, or other names. This person is seen as the expert in dealing with this impersonal spiritual power. When animists want something special done—good or evil—they go to the shaman because he or she knows how to *manipulate* this power. This kind of belief (hiring a shaman, participating in the rituals, and living by the shaman's advice) is found in all parts of the world and is basic to many cultures.

Spirit beings are the second source of spiritual power for animists. They're believed to have individual identities and functions, knowingly engaging in good or evil actions. They may be associated with objects in nature, or the spirits of people who have died. Or they may be seen in a whole variety of other ways. As with *mana*, spirits also are thought to be controllable to some extent by humans who know the right things to do, words to say, and objects to use. But the control is not absolute, and this lack of control causes animists to

53

live in constant fear of displeasing the spirits and incurring their wrath. They also fear that an enemy may be using some superior occult skill to direct the power of *mana* or the power of the spirits against them. For the animist, almost everything in life is related in some way to the spirit world. We could say that they see *everything* as spiritual and supernatural.

So for the animist, biblical accounts of Satan and his demons are easily interpreted through the filter of their worldview. Incidentally, the worldview of the people in biblical times was much closer to animism than it was to our secularized Western worldview.

The Western Worldview: Nothing Is Supernatural

Because the West has become so multicultural, there is no one "Western worldview." But there are some things that can be said about the worldview with which most Westerners (people in Europe and the Americas) have grown up. The Western worldview is generally divided into two functional realms: the supernatural realm and the natural realm. In the supernatural realm are placed all spirit beings, including God, angels, and demons, because they are supernatural and don't fit into the natural world dominated by scientific thinking. This supernatural realm is seen as basically unimportant, and so far removed from the natural realm that the two not only are separate; they don't even touch. Spiritual issues are considered unnecessary for understanding life.

The natural realm is thought to be governed by scientific laws. Even for those Westerners who believe that God may have created the world and established the laws that govern it, He is now seen as seated on His throne in heaven, seldom

Western Worldview

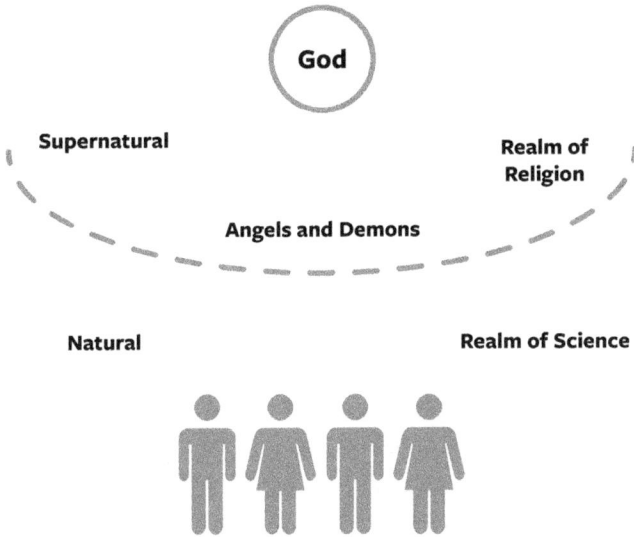

God

Supernatural

Realm of
Religion

Angels and Demons

Natural

Realm of Science

interfering with life on earth. Occasionally, we experience a "miracle," but that's the exception, not the rule. The general assumption is that religion and science don't interact and should be kept separate.

Based on this worldview, people tend to ask "either-or" questions: "Is this a matter of religion or a matter of science?" "Is this a private (spiritual) or public (scientific) consideration?" But the question heard most often is, "How do you know whether a person's problem is spiritual or psychological?" That's an invalid question because it's based on an invalid worldview. God created each of us as a whole person, with all our parts intricately related to each other. That includes the body, soul (*psyche*), and spirit. The *psyche* cannot be reduced to something that is explained scientifically. It's part of the image of God in a person and can only be properly understood in that light.

Body, soul, and spirit constantly interact. Only from a perverted Western worldview do we try to explain life without reference to God and the reality of the spirit world. Trying to resolve spiritual problems by physical means will never work. Taking a pill to help cure your body may be commendable, but taking a pill to cure the soul is deplorable. A biblical worldview sees the need for the pastor as well as the doctor.

About three hundred years ago in Western culture, the worldview was quite different. Theology was considered "the queen of the sciences." Everything was tested by agreement with the truth revealed in the Bible. It was assumed back then that this is a created world and that God speaks both through His creation and through His Word. The physical world could be properly understood only as God's work and revelation to us.

The Enlightenment brought strong philosophical voices that said humankind did not get significance from a relationship to some supernatural person, but from an ability to reason. Then the scientific revolution added the concept that only the scientific method was a reliable method of finding truth. Later, the theory of evolution was also added to this philosophical mix. Since the world was assumed to have evolved rather than been created, we could no longer see it as a channel of God's revelation.

This Enlightenment worldview not only eliminated God from any functional relationship to life on earth; it also eliminated the idea of angels and demons. Such spirit beings had no place in the thinking of this worldview. This view became so pervasive in the West that even theologians and pastors were influenced by it. With this secularized Western worldview in the Church, it's no wonder that spiritual warfare is seldom addressed in the Church or even in Christian education. It also becomes clear why worldview is such a crucial topic in discussing spiritual warfare. The animist worldview is that everything is spiritual; the Western worldview is that nothing important is spiritual.

The Biblical Worldview

The worldview taught by the prophets and apostles of God's Word is the one we need to adopt. The biblical worldview has three realms: the realm of God alone, the realm of angels, and the realm of people and things. When we talk about these realms, we are not talking about places, but realms of being. God is certainly not limited to a place far away in outer space. He is present everywhere in His creation. But God is the one Being in the realm of deity—not God and the angels, or anything else.

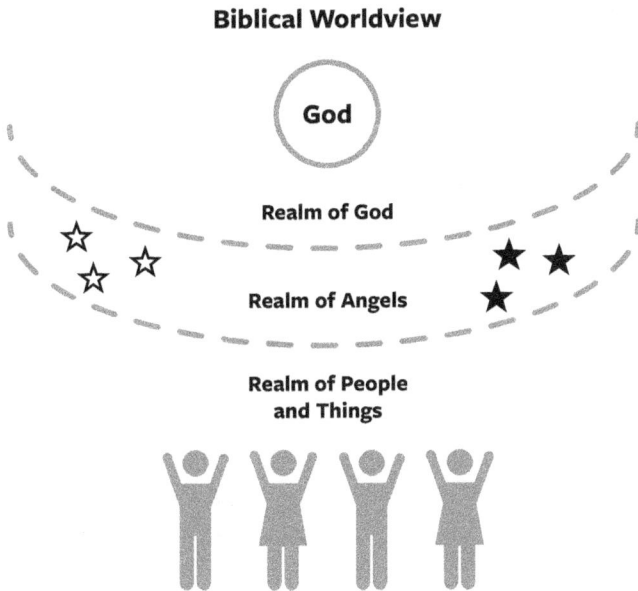

Biblical Worldview

God

Realm of God

Realm of Angels

Realm of People and Things

The realm of angels is the one Westerners have problems with. They prefer not to see spirit beings as functional parts of our world because their existence in our material world is incompatible with Enlightenment thinking and scientific materialism. Hence, all spirit beings are assigned to the supernatural realm.

However, as the world came from the creative hand of God, the realm of angels was fully populated. There were angels—cherubs, seraphim, archangels, principalities, powers—a dozen or so terms used in the Bible for the angels. Angels worship God in heaven and carry out His orders in relation to His creation and to people on earth. It was obviously a good arrangement; it came from the hand of God. God Himself pronounced it "very good."

It just did not stay "very good" when one of the highest angels decided to lead a rebellion against God and His authority. We don't have a straight narrative of what happened, but it appears that Lucifer decided he wanted to be equal to God. He apparently persuaded a whole group of angels to join him in his revolt. We often refer to these as "fallen angels." We see Satan trying to act like God when he tempted Jesus to worship him (see Luke 4:5–7). Paul tells us that at the end of this age Satan will come in "the man of sin" (2 Thessalonians 2:3 KJV) and "exalt himself over everything that is called God or is worshiped, so that he sets himself up in God's temple, proclaiming himself to be God" (verse 4). He seems to have one great ambition: to be God, or at least to be like God. He knows now that he will never make that goal (see Revelation 12:12), so he is committed to opposing all of God's purposes for the rest of creation.

Satan's primary issue with God seems to be the fact that God has all the glory and he has none. His objective seems to be to grab glory for himself and to deprive God of His glory. He can't launch a frontal attack on the throne of God, but he can cause God's people on earth to fail to glorify God in their bodies.

In the Ten Commandments, God commanded Israel, as His chosen people, not to bear His name in vain (see Exodus 20:7). We understand this to mean that we should not use the Lord's name as a curse. While that is certainly part of the meaning, God was also talking about His people being called His children but not living in a way that would bring Him glory. If we profess Christ but live like we belong to the devil, it shames God's name.

Israel lived among the "nations"—those who did not know the God of Israel. God had planned for the Gentiles to know Him by the way Israel lived in obedience to Him and trusted Him. That way, God could reveal Himself *through Israel* to other nations. The Gentiles would look at Israel and say, "We don't know a God like yours." But when Israel did not live to the glory of God, that message was not conveyed. Israel bore the name "children of God" *in vain.*

In the New Testament, Paul tells us that "whether you eat or drink or *whatever* you do, do it all for the glory of God" (1 Corinthians 10:31, emphasis added). To call ourselves children of God but not live in a way that reflects His glory is to bear the Lord's name in vain, which gives Satan satisfaction. The idea of pleasing Satan rather than God should be enough motivation for us to live God-honoring lives!

The Warfare Worldview

The major thrust of spiritual warfare is not the more sensational types of demonic manifestations. The primary battle is over control of our minds, hearts, and daily lives. The problem is that if our worldview doesn't include a correct view of God and doesn't see Satan as a functional part of this struggle, we will wrestle with flesh and blood and forget that we are also spiritual beings wrestling with principalities and powers (see Ephesians 6:12).

We can't fully understand the Bible and its message without coming to terms with the warfare worldview. By a warfare worldview, we mean that the cosmic battle between the Kingdom of God and the kingdom of Satan is a real battle. God in His sovereignty has guaranteed the outcome of the war, but the battles we fight from day to day require us to use the minds and wills He has given us and to use the armor and weapons He provides.

A biblical worldview is based on the sovereignty of God. He is the ultimate source of power in this universe. He is, in fact, the *only* source of power. He has delegated power to angels and to men, but He is the source of that power. Both angels and men may misuse the power they have been given, but they do not *produce* power apart from God's creative action.

Many worldviews include other sources of power—an impersonal kind of power, various kinds of spirits, or even man as his own god. In animism, the god is certainly not sovereign. In the West, God is often treated like one who created the world but now pays no attention to its operation. Unless we see God as the only sovereign source of power, we will continue to look to other sources for the power we think we need. If we say we hold the biblical worldview but read the horoscope or call the psychic hotline, we show by our actions that we don't believe God is the sovereign source of power.

Filter Free

Our worldview is the filter through which we will understand spiritual warfare. It's also clear that the biblical worldview is essential if we are to live to the glory of God and be "more than conquerors" in Christ. In Colossians 2:8–10, Paul shows the contrast between the biblical worldview and any other worldview that opposes it:

> See to it that no one takes you captive through hollow and deceptive philosophy, which depends on human tradition and the elemental spiritual forces of this world rather than on Christ.
>
> For in Christ all the fullness of the Deity lives in bodily form, and in Christ you have been brought to fullness. He is the head over every power and authority.

This is also what Paul had in mind when he commanded, "Do not conform to the pattern of this world, but be transformed by the renewing of your mind" (Romans 12:2). A biblical worldview is essential for a renewed mind. It is also a necessary ingredient in understanding spiritual warfare and in fighting the battles victoriously.

FIVE

Know Your Enemy

We live in a day of quick fixes—fast food, microwave dinners, tap and pay, the Internet. In the fast-paced world of the twenty-first century, it's very tempting to try to find a quick fix for our personal and spiritual problems. Without minimizing the possibility of God intervening in our lives at times of special need with His own miraculous "quick fix," it's safe to say that He usually expects us to use the resources He has given us to work through the problems of life. He made us in His image, with the ability to think, feel, and make decisions, and He encourages us to use those abilities.

A great picture is that of a person at the helm of a ship, the Lord standing beside the individual as a mentor, with His hand on his or her shoulder. There are indeed some things that only God can do—things like creating something out of nothing, sustaining the universe with the word of His power, defining truth, and providing redemption for fallen humankind. There are some things, however, that God has equipped us to do, and He will be there to help us and to mentor us, but He will not excuse us from our part.

God does not fill our minds with a knowledge of His Word. We read it, study it, memorize it, meditate on it, and obey it. We put on the armor that He has provided for us. We meet the changing circumstances of our lives with the resources that are available to us as children whom He loves. We use our ability to make decisions. He will help us with the process and correct us when we make bad decisions, but He will never tell us to be passive. Even in our waiting, we are actively praying, actively listening, alert and prepared.

We live in a fallen world, and our Lord has told us very clearly that "in this world you will have trouble" (John 16:33). Fortunately for us, Jesus goes on to say in the same verse, "But take heart! I have overcome the world." The promise of victory, however, does not excuse us from the trouble. It is like what we hear God tell His people in the Old Testament:

> When you pass through the waters, I will be with you; and when you pass through the rivers, they will not sweep over you. When you walk through the fire, you will not be burned; the flames will not set you ablaze.
>
> Isaiah 43:2

God's people were not promised that they wouldn't go through the floods and the fire. They were simply given the assurance that God would be with them at such times.

So today, we expect to face difficult situations. Even for Jesus, this was so: "Son though he was, he learned obedience from what he suffered" (Hebrews 5:8). Times of suffering are not all the work of Satan in a direct sense. He is ultimately the source of all that is evil, but although he introduced the corrupting influences into the world, let's not give him more credit or more attention than he deserves. Let's not excuse ourselves from doing the things God has commissioned us to do.

In being self-controlled in the use of our minds, God expects us to think, not just let anything in that happens to wander through. He encourages us to use what reflects His image in us, and those qualities include our minds and our wills. This is not to say that God doesn't guide us. He does, but as we heard both Peter and Paul tell us, we need to be "self-controlled and alert."

It should be noted here that mental passivity is one of the most dangerous things we can do, spiritually. It opens us to Satan's deception. But in our quest for quick fixes, we may revert to the idea that if we can just locate the right demon to exorcise, we can solve almost any problem. While it's true that there is some spiritual dimension to all human predicaments, it's seldom true that our problem is simply a matter of dealing with a demon.

We have had people ask us if we do exorcisms, because they had a demon they wanted to get rid of. The standard answer to such people is, "I have only Christian answers to human problems. If you are interested in seeking God's answers for your life, I am interested in helping you. But if you simply want to get rid of a demon so that you can get on with your own agenda for your life, I cannot promise you any help."

What Is Spiritual Warfare?

If spiritual warfare is not just going around rebuking the devil and getting rid of demons, what is it? The primary location of that battle is *our minds*. Either we believe the lies that keep us in bondage, or we choose to believe the truth that sets us free. Spiritual warfare is primarily the battle for the mind.

Our abilities to think, feel, and make decisions (our minds, emotions, and wills) are intricately linked together. Yet our thoughts generally determine how we feel and how we act. It often appears that emotions are the determining factor, but emotions are only as valid as the truth on which they are based. They may lead to significant action, but emotions are rooted in what we think about the circumstances of life, even if the thoughts aren't accurate.

Every action is just a product of our thoughts. "For as he thinks within himself, so he is" (Proverbs 23:7 NASB). The will and emotions can act only on what the mind knows. Wrong information, lack of knowledge, or a faulty belief system can lead to undesirable and even destructive actions. Satan knows this, and this explains why deception is his primary tactic. This is also why Peter tells us to "prepare your minds for action; be self-controlled" (1 Peter 1:13 NIV1984). He wants us to understand that if we can win the battle for the mind, we can win the battle against Satan the deceiver.

But the battle for the mind is mainly a matter of having a *functioning faith* based on truth. There is a fundamental difference between the brain and the mind. The brain is an organism that the mind uses. To put it in computer terms, the brain is the hardware, and the mind is the software. One can have a perfectly functioning computer, but if the software program has bugs in it, the results can be disastrous. In computer language, it's "garbage in, garbage out." When a computer is not programmed to handle data properly, there is no value to its calculation. In the same way, the human brain functions only according to how it has been programmed.

Life comes down to the principle that if we believe right we will live right, but we need to understand that right belief is more than right *knowledge*.

More Than Profession

There's a saying, "What you do hollers so loud I can't hear what you say."

This is a principle of life we've seen already: People may not live what they profess, but they will always live what they believe. This is what Jesus meant when He said, "By their fruit you will recognize them" (Matthew 7:20).

Our *profession* of what we believe is often based on truth—what we've read or learned—and there is nothing wrong with that kind of learning. But *life-changing* belief is based on Spirit-taught truth.

Profession is what we know with our brains. Belief is what has found a home *in our hearts*. That's why Paul says that you can and should be "transformed by the renewing of your mind" (Romans 12:2).

The Master Deceiver

Satan does not want that transforming process to take place. He knows that if he can control what we believe, he can control how we live. Dictators and cult leaders have used this tactic for years, but it began with the devil himself. Paul said that with evil leaders it is a case of "deceiving and being deceived" (2 Timothy 3:13). Satan first deceives the leaders, and then they in turn deceive others. Saying they were deceived does not excuse them.

Satan's temptation of Adam and Eve in the garden was to suggest to them that God could not be trusted, that He had told them something that was not true. Then Satan appealed to their self-interest in suggesting that they could become like God. Satan had become the fiend that he was by trying to be like God (see Isaiah 14:12–15; Matthew 4:9; 2 Thessalonians 2:4). Now he was suggesting that possibility to the man and woman God had created in His own image.

It's interesting to speculate on what might have happened if Adam had been involved at the start, or if Adam and Eve had talked this over. We are thus introduced to another of Satan's tactics—namely, to isolate us and approach us when we are *alone*. He will say, "You should be able to handle this by yourself. You shouldn't have to consult God or anyone else." Besides isolation, this calls attention to another of Satan's tactics—*urgency*: "Do it right now—no time to think it over!"

If such deception could happen in a perfect place like the garden of Eden, it certainly can happen to us in the fallen world in which we live. That's why Jesus prayed, "My prayer is not that you take them out of the world but that you protect them from the evil one. They are not of the world, even as I am not of it. Sanctify them by the truth; your word is truth" (John 17:15–17). We don't overcome the father of lies by human reasoning or scientific research; only by the truth revealed to us in the Bible.

The World, the Flesh, and the Devil

Discussions of spiritual warfare sooner or later get around to asking what the relationship is between the world, the flesh, and the devil. Paul introduces all three elements into his definitive statement about this warfare:

And you were dead in your offenses and sins, in which you previously walked according to the course of this world, according to the prince of the power of the air, of the spirit that is now working in the sons of disobedience. Among them we too all previously lived in the lusts of our flesh, indulging the desires of the flesh and of the mind, and were by nature children of wrath, just as the rest.

Ephesians 2:1–3 NASB

Notice the way Paul links the world, the flesh, and the devil together. He does not suggest that sometimes it's the world we are dealing with, sometimes the flesh, and sometimes the devil. Paul sees them as working so closely together that you really can't understand one without seeing the way it relates to the others. The biblical terms *world* (*kosmos*) and *flesh* (*sarx*) can have very different meanings. But there is very little ambiguity about Satan's identity!

The Greek word *kosmos* is used with two very different meanings. Satan is called the "prince" (NIV) or "ruler" (NASB) of this world (*kosmos*) by Jesus (see John 12:31; 14:30; 16:11), and we are commanded not to love the world (see 1 John 2:15) in this sense.

In some measure, Satan created the world we see—the world of fallen human culture. And he is the ruler of that world. This was not the world as it came from the creative hand of God. God created the world, and He rules over that creation (see Colossians 1:17; Hebrews 1:3). The physical world reveals God's glory, and it's part of what God has given us to enjoy (see 1 Timothy 6:17). The world of people God created is another proper object of our love. God Himself "so loved the world [of people] that he gave his one and only Son, that whoever believes in him shall not perish but have eternal life" (John 3:16). Thus, the world as God created it is good. It is not our enemy.

When we speak of the world in the context of the world, the flesh, and the devil, we are talking about the world full of things designed by Satan to tempt us to meet our legitimate human needs in a way never intended by the Creator. They are the deceptions Satan has devised to get us to make bad decisions, just as Eve did in the garden. With that first bad decision—to listen to Satan rather than to God—a process was begun that has resulted in human cultures that have moved far from the Creator. It began with one person and one decision. It spread to two people, and gradually embraced the world. So in that sense, the *world* is a carefully crafted scheme of Satan to lead people away from God and His good purposes for them and into bondage to the lies of an enemy.

This is the world to which we as God's people are no longer to conform. In Romans 12:2, Paul puts this in the form of a strong command that could be translated "Stop conforming to the world!" We live our lives in the context of this world, but, as Jesus put it in His High Priestly Prayer, we are not to be "of the world" (John 17:16). In a sense, sanctification is the process of freeing ourselves from and keeping ourselves free from the corruption of the world. That is a key idea in Jesus' prayer for us in John 17.

It is also significant that when Jesus prays about our relationship to the world, He links the world and the devil when He says, "My prayer is not that you take them out of the world but that you protect them from *the evil one*" (John 17:15, emphasis added). The idea that sometimes we are just dealing with the world misses the fact that Satan is the one who fabricated these temptations and who is pushing us to yield to them. Jesus seemed to assume this relationship when He taught His disciples to pray, "Lead us not into temptation, but deliver us *from the evil one*" (Matthew 6:13, emphasis added). We are told to avoid, even to "flee" from, places and circumstances that lead to temptation (see 1 Corinthians 6:18; 1 Timothy 6:11; 2 Timothy 2:22), but when temptation is happening, we are to resist the enemy (see Ephesians 6:11; James 4:7; 1 Peter 5:9).

Satan is smart enough not to make himself too obvious. He often comes as an angel of light, or he sends his henchmen dressed as "ministers of righteousness" (2 Corinthians 11:15 KJV). Deception is his game.

Paul uses the image of a trap in writing to Timothy. Traps are set to deceive animals into thinking that something good—the bait—is available to them, without recognizing how it's attached to a trigger that will spring the trap. Paul says that some people in the Church have fallen into the "trap of the devil" and are doing what he wants rather than what God wants. They have fallen for the bait that there is a way other than God's to meet their legitimate needs. Paul makes it clear that the way out of the trap is "the truth" (2 Timothy 2:25–26). The fact that truth is the way out of the trap implies that lies are the trap. We are deceived into thinking we can sin without having to suffer the consequences.

But what about the flesh? In Galatians 5, Paul says the struggle is between spirit and flesh, not between spirit and Satan. James tells us that we are drawn away by our own desires, not by a demon (see James 1:13–15). Yes, the battle is fought at the level of our flesh.

Let's define *flesh* carefully. There are at least eight different meanings for the Greek word *sarx* (flesh). While this may sound a bit intimidating, there is a sense in which the meanings all relate to one primary idea. This idea is that we are human beings with physical bodies, living in a time-space world. The word *flesh* can mean things related to or part of the body, like flesh and bones. Yet we are more than just bodies. We also have personalities that identify us as individuals. Our personalities are made up of our ability to think, feel, and make decisions. The term *flesh* is used to incorporate all these ideas. In a sense, it's simply a way of saying we are *human*. The problem is, the flesh (our humanness) is weak and is conditioned to operate independently of God. It is hostile to the Spirit of God at work in us (see Galatians 5:16–17). That means we must be totally dependent on God.

We are spiritual beings who are created in the image of God. This is part of what it is to be human, and these human qualities require resources to sustain them. The body needs food and water. As persons or personalities, we need to feel significant, secure, and accepted. We need to love and be loved. As spiritual beings, we need a relationship with God. It is these needs that are in view when James says that we are drawn away by our own *desires*. We have needs that we desire to have met. This should happen as intended by our Creator. These needs and the desire to meet them were present in the garden of Eden before sin entered the picture. Desires are not bad. They don't constitute a sinful nature. They were there when God created Adam and Eve. Needs or desires themselves may not be wrong (see Matthew 13:17; Luke 22:15; Philippians 1:23; 1 Thessalonians 2:17).

But Satan often suggests how those desires can be met in ways contrary to what God intends. We have noted how human cultures have tended to degenerate spiritually so that the *world* today is often an enemy of Christian growth and maturity. In a similar manner, our flesh has been programmed to live independently of God.

After the Fall, Adam and Eve had lost their relationship with God, so they sought to find identity and purpose for life apart from God. Learning to live our lives independently of God is what led to the downward course of human culture. *Culture* may be defined as "learned and shared human behavior." Almost everything that we humans do is learned. We come into this life able to learn, and we can pass on that learning. Human beings can write books and teach others what they have learned, and that's what produces what we call culture. Culture is the accumulation of learned ideas and behaviors—good and bad—passed from one generation to the next within societies that share a common heritage. Our modern cultures are the result of learning and cultural borrowing from places and peoples all over the world. It's essentially the part of culture that passes on learned evil that the Bible calls "the world."

Most societies place a high priority on having their members conform to the accepted cultural beliefs and practices of those societies. A popular term for this is *peer pressure*, which functions to promote what is good, but also can promote what is evil. This is the negative connotation of what the Bible calls "the world." It is a world that has unfortunately taken its lead in trying to meet human needs and desires from the god of this world rather than from the one true Creator God.

The world tells us that our needs and desires can be met with the counterfeits that Satan has suggested, and people everywhere try to meet their needs this way. When James describes how we are drawn away by our own *desires* (NIV) or *lusts* (KJV), it is indeed our basic human needs that provide the possibility of our being drawn away. These needs or desires have acquired a negative connotation here because of the way we have tried to meet them through Satan's supermarket of wrong choices. It's not the desires that are wrong; it's the way we have tried to meet them. And just as Jesus linked temptation and the tempter in the prayer He taught His disciples (see Matthew 6:9–13), so we need to see that relationship implied in the idea of being *drawn away*. It is Satan who is the mastermind behind that strategy. He is the one who does the drawing away by suggesting all the deceptive alternatives to us when we try to meet our legitimate needs.

So in talking about the world, the flesh, and the devil, we need to understand that it is not all one or all the other. Most of the time, it is not even mostly one or the other. They work together, and we need a strategy for resistance that considers all three. We all have needs. The question is, are those needs going to be met by the world, the flesh, and the devil, or by Christ, who promises to meet all our needs according to His riches in glory (see Philippians 4:19)?

Our deepest needs are met by Jesus Christ, as illustrated in the lists that follow:

"In Christ" I am accepted . . .

John 1:12	I am God's child.
John 15:15	I am Christ's friend.
Romans 5:1	I have been justified.
1 Corinthians 6:17	I am united with the Lord.
1 Corinthians 6:19–20	I have been bought with a price. I belong to God.
1 Corinthians 12:27	I am a member of Christ's body.
Ephesians 1:1	I am a saint.
Ephesians 1:5	I have been adopted as God's child.
Ephesians 2:18	I have direct access to God through the Holy Spirit.
Colossians 1:14	I have been redeemed and forgiven.
Colossians 2:10	I am complete in Christ.

"In Christ" I am secure . . .

Romans 8:1–2	I am free forever from condemnation.
Romans 8:28	I am assured that all things work together for good.
Romans 8:31–34	I am free from any condemning charges against me.
Romans 8:35–39	I cannot be separated from the love of God.
2 Corinthians 1:21–22	I have been established, anointed, and sealed by God.
Philippians 1:6	I am confident the good work God has begun in me will be perfected.
Philippians 3:20	I am a citizen of heaven.
Colossians 3:3	I am hidden with Christ in God.
2 Timothy 1:7	I have not been given a spirit of fear, but of power, love, and a sound mind.
Hebrews 4:16	I can find grace and mercy in time of need.
1 John 5:18	I am born of God, and the evil one cannot touch me.

"In Christ" I am significant . . .

Matthew 5:13–14	I am the salt of the earth.
John 15:1, 5	I am a branch of the true vine, a channel of His life.
John 15:16	I have been chosen and appointed to bear fruit.
Acts 1:8	I am a personal witness of Christ.
1 Corinthians 3:16	I am God's temple.
2 Corinthians 5:17–21	I am a minister of reconciliation for God.
2 Corinthians 6:1	I am God's co-worker (see also 1 Corinthians 3:9).
Ephesians 2:6	I am seated with Christ in the heavenly realms.
Ephesians 2:10	I am God's workmanship.
Ephesians 3:12	I may approach God with freedom and confidence.
Philippians 4:13	I can do all things through Christ who strengthens me.

Paul says you can be "*transformed* by the renewing of your mind" (Romans 12:2, emphasis added). But the enemy has convinced some that they cannot change. "That's just the way I am," they say. Or "It works for others, but not for me." Remember, Satan is a deceiver. The idea that you cannot do something God tells you to do has to be a lie from our enemy. God doesn't command us to do things we cannot do. He doesn't tell us that we can be victors in *most things*, but that we are powerless against some of the enemy's attacks. He tells us that we are "more than conquerors" (Romans 8:37). Paul doesn't say, "I can do most things through Christ who strengthens me." He says, "I can do all things through Him who strengthens me" (Philippians 4:13 NASB). The problem is (we'll say it again!) that we will always *live* what we really *believe*, and if we believe we cannot do something, we won't even try.

Satan has kept many people from spiritual growth and maturity with this tactic. We listen when he suggests thoughts to our minds like, *The idea of spiritual victory and fruitfulness is fine for others, but I'm too weak. I just don't have enough faith.* Or the thought, *I guess the devil has my number. He knows that I just can't resist in that area.* Or, *I just don't feel that way, and if I do something I don't feel like doing, I'm a hypocrite.* Notice that Satan will phrase such thoughts as though they were your own. If he can convince you that you really believe something, you will begin to act on that belief.

Perhaps you are asking, "If Satan can put thoughts into my mind, wouldn't that be like saying, 'The devil made me do it'?" The answer is yes, Satan can put thoughts into our minds, and no, it's not like saying the devil made you do it. The Scriptures tell us that Satan put thoughts in the minds of David, Judas, and Ananias (see 1 Chronicles 21:1; John 13:2; Acts 5:3). The devil even put thoughts in Jesus' mind. One day, Jesus had this thought in His mind: *If you bow down and worship Satan, he will give you all the kingdoms of the world.* What a horrible thing for Him to be thinking! Where did that thought come from? It obviously was not from Jesus' own thinking. It came from the devil, who was tempting Him. The Bible says that Jesus was "tempted in every way, *just as we are*" (Hebrews 4:15, emphasis added).

The devil is a spiritual being, and Jesus had taken on the form of a man (see Philippians 2:7). But the communication was from a spirit to a person. That's the way temptation happens; Jesus was tempted just the way we are. If it happened to Jesus, believe that it can happen to us.

Being tempted, however, is not sin. We cannot prevent temptation, but we can resist temptation. That's why it's never correct to say, "The devil made me do it." We are always responsible for what we allow into our minds and for what we do with the encouragements to evil that are all around us. At the same time, to deny that Satan is involved in the process is to fail to deal with a critical element in any temptation.

Of course, Satan is only a fallen angel, to be sure. He would like to have us believe that he is stronger than God, but that simply isn't so, and we should never ascribe the attributes of deity to him. He depends on his demonic hierarchy to carry out his nefarious schemes. This is what was behind Martin Luther's famous words "And though this world with devils filled should threaten to undo us, we will not fear, for God hath willed his truth to triumph through us." Satan and his host of fallen angels are everywhere in "the world," but that should not cause us alarm, because God has given us the truth as our primary defense against their deceitful attacks.

We all have our share of spiritual conflict. We have our share of trouble. They go together. If Satan doesn't cause the trouble, he will try to take advantage of it when it comes to us. Living in a fallen world produces plenty of trouble without Satan starting something new. He is an opportunist, on hand to make the trouble seem even worse than it is, and to make you feel so much like a victim that you will begin to act like a victim rather than like a victor in Christ. The battle is for the mind. It is a battle of truth versus lies. If we can win that battle, we can win all the others.

Knowing the Outcome

In most wars, the winner is not often predetermined—at least not from the standpoint of the people involved. But the spiritual war in which we are involved is one we already know will end. We know God will win. We need to distinguish between the battles that make up the war and the war itself. We may lose some battles, but the outcome of the war is no longer in doubt. Christ determined that outcome when He paid the penalty for our sin at the cross and when He conquered death by rising from the tomb. The writer to the Hebrews puts it this way:

> Since the children [that's you and me] have flesh and blood, he too shared in their humanity so that *by his death he might break the power of him who holds the power of death*—that is, the devil—and free those who all their lives were held in slavery by their fear of death.
>
> Hebrews 2:14–15, emphasis added

We can even say that we have all the resources we need to win every battle. The only question is whether we will fight the battle the Lord's way, using the weapons, armor, and strategy that He gives. This principle is illustrated in the battles Israel fought with their enemies in the Old Testament. When they acted in faith and obedience, they always won, no matter how lopsided the military odds seemed.

Gideon is a great example of this. When the angel of the Lord called Gideon to lead the forces of Israel, Gideon said,

"How can I save Israel? My clan is the weakest in Manasseh, and I am the least in my family" (Judges 6:15).

The angel reminded him that the issue was not who *he* was, but who *God* is. "Do things God's way," the angel in effect prompted him, "and God will be responsible for the results."

Gideon chose to obey. With three hundred men armed only with torches, clay pots, and trumpets, they routed the whole army of the Midianites (see Judges 6–7).

When the Israelites didn't bother to consult God before a battle and tried to figure things out for themselves, they always lost. At Ai, for example, they did their demographic study and made their strategic decision based on their own evaluation. Much to their surprise, they were soundly defeated by the men of the little village of Ai. The Israelites did things their way, apparently without even asking God about it, and they got what their way could produce (see Joshua 7–8).

This principle continues to operate in the warfare we are engaged in today. Do things God's way, and God will be responsible for the results. Do things our way, and we must be responsible for the results.

So if the outcome of the battle we fight depends on our doing things God's way, we need to make certain that our relationship with the Lord is intimate, and free of distraction or disruption. We need to make certain that we are in touch with Him through a knowledge of His Word and a meaningful prayer life.

Technique or Magic?

Spiritual warfare is not a question of saying the right words, doing the right things, using the right objects, praying the right prayers. This is magical thinking—much like what a shaman would do. Those who practice magic assume that there is a power that can be manipulated by using the right techniques. (Remember animism?) But we cannot manipulate God!

In our technological age, we may not think in terms of magic, but rather tech support—manuals or videos. But the Bible is not an instruction book we get with things; an instruction book tells us how to handle an *object*. The Bible tells us how to *relate to the Creator* of objects.

If Americans had fought the battle of Jericho, we would have appointed a task force to write a manual on "How to Take a Double-Walled City." The only problem is that if such a manual had been written based on the Israelites' experience, it would never have been useful, because God made His people come back to Him *personally* for new instructions for *every* new battle. There may be something to learn from a previous battle, but winning our battle with Satan is not a matter of technique, but of *relationship*. Our relationship with our Lord is basic to understanding and dealing with our relationship with the enemy. Let's look at these relationships.

Warfare Relationships

The biblical worldview we have already described shows us the key relationships in our spiritual warfare. Beginning with the concept of the three functional realms of being—God, angels, and people—we note that people are believers or unbelievers. Believers have exercised saving faith in the fact that Christ bore the penalty for all their sin when He died on the cross. Unbelievers have not done this. The only basis for our relationship with God is through His amazing grace. He planned for this before He even created us (see Ephesians

1:4–5), and He initiated the action that made it possible (see Revelation 13:8). It is made effective as we receive it by faith (see Ephesians 2:8–9). Acting in faith brings us into a whole new relationship with God.

Now let's take a brief look at the relationship between Satan and both unbelievers and believers, as explained in the Bible. We know Satan's primary tactic is deception. We are told in Revelation 12:9 that he "deceives the whole world" (NKJV). Deception is his means of control over people. John tells us that "the whole world is under the control of the evil one" (1 John 5:19). Paul says that the unsaved person follows "the ways of this world and of the ruler of the kingdom of the air" (Ephesians 2:2). If someone deceives you, you don't

Satan and Unbelievers

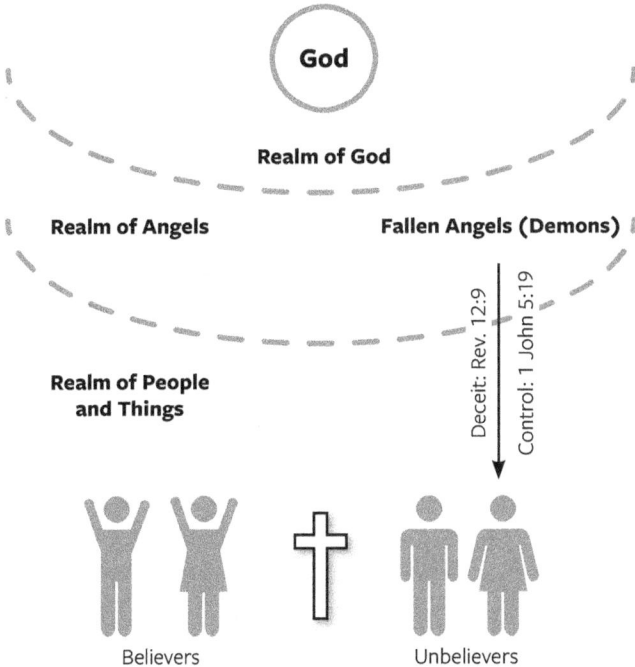

God

Realm of God

Realm of Angels   Fallen Angels (Demons)

Deceit: Rev. 12:9   Control: 1 John 5:19

Realm of People
and Things

Believers   Unbelievers

81

know it. If you knew it, you wouldn't be deceived! You accept what you're being told and act on it.

We said before that dictators and cult leaders have used this strategy since Satan introduced it in the garden. People do bizarre things once they fall for a deception. Satan has developed his lies so cleverly that we don't even think that what he says may be a lie. When we recognize the deception, at times our pride keeps us from admitting it. Yes, deception is an effective means of control.

There is only one lie Satan tells unbelievers to control them: That there is a way to find true life other than through the cross of Christ. Satan hates the cross. There, he was disarmed (see Colossians 2:15) and ultimately destroyed (see Hebrews 2:14–15). Satan is not the enemy of religion. He will suggest any kind of a religious idea if he thinks he can use it to keep people from the cross.

Paul tells us that "the god of this age has blinded the minds of unbelievers, so that they cannot see the light of the gospel that displays the glory of Christ, who is the image of God" (2 Corinthians 4:4). A deceived person believes a lie and is thus blind to the truth. Satan doesn't care how close you come to the truth—as long as you miss it. This is why he likes to appear as an angel of light or as a servant of righteousness (see 2 Corinthians 11:13–15). When people think they are being very religious in what they believe or what they do, they assume that they must be right. "Just so you are sincere," the enemy will say. "Religion is a very personal thing. You have to discover what is true for you."

Satan has been very successful at this. There are religious systems of all kinds, and some people believe that any of them will get you to your desired goal. It's socially acceptable today to talk about spirituality, but not to believe that

God has spoken authoritatively in the Scriptures and in the Person of His Son. So the whole unbelieving world indeed "is under the control of the evil one" (1 John 5:19), kept there with a simple lie.

Since we're here to discuss the spiritual warfare of the believer, let's consider the relationship between Satan and the believer. When a person comes to the cross and moves from Satan's camp into God's camp, a lot of things change. Paul says that such a person becomes a "new creation," and that "the old has gone, the new is here!" (2 Corinthians 5:17). One thing that doesn't change, however, is Satan's tactic. He is still the liar and deceiver he has always been (see John 8:44;

Satan's Relationship to the Believer

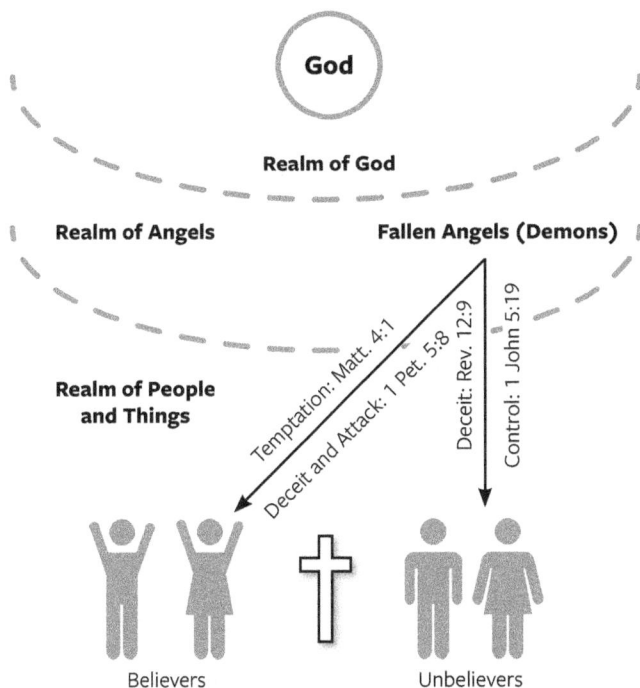

$$God$$

Realm of God

Realm of Angels   Fallen Angels (Demons)

Realm of People
and Things

Temptation: Matt. 4:1

Deceit and Attack: 1 Pet. 5:8

Deceit: Rev. 12:9

Control: 1 John 5:19

Believers   Unbelievers

Revelation 12:9). We don't get immunity to his lies by following Christ. Usually, he steps up his attacks considerably, because now we have the capacity to live to the glory of God (see 1 Corinthians 10:31), and the potential to help people move from Satan's kingdom into God's Kingdom. Satan is therefore more concerned with neutralizing the child of God than with harassing those who are already in his own kingdom.

We use the term *neutralize* intentionally. Satan knows that he is not going to get many believers to renounce their faith and turn away from the Lord. But he also knows that he can deceive us so that we won't live in a way that will bring glory to God—and we won't resist our enemy "in the faith" (1 Peter 5:9). He neutralizes us! No, we aren't worshiping him, but we aren't hurting him either. We may be more comfortable far away from the battle, but it's not the way to fight a war.

When a person begins to get serious about serving the Lord, attacks can be expected to increase. We could say that the Christian is the devil's target, but those actively involved in ministry are the bull's-eye. Sometimes people ask, "Before I was really sold out to the Lord and seeking to serve Him, I didn't have the problems I have now. How come?"

The answer is, "Welcome to the war. When you get up on the front lines of battle, expect to be shot at."

The problem often is that because of Satan's deceptive tactics, his attacks are not recognized as such. It's not correct to see the devil behind *every* problem, but neither is it correct *not* to see his involvement in the problem.

Power Source

Satan is a powerful angel. For whatever reason, God did not withdraw the power delegated to him after he rebelled against Him. But we can be sure his power is limited. God is the source of all power, and He delegates that power as He sees fit. Satan tries to make us think he is as powerful as God. People who have been involved in Satan worship bear witness to this deception among the followers of Satan.

Satan is like an animal on a tether. The animal can go as far as the tether allows, but no farther. He can act freely within the area defined by his rope, but the rope defines his area of activity. Satan is on God's tether, and while he can do many things within the limited area defined by God, he certainly cannot go beyond the limits God has established. If he could, he would have reduced God's creation to chaos long ago. He is not happy that "the heavens declare the glory of God" (Psalm 19:1) and that God's children can live to the glory of God.

Although his power is limited, Satan can do supernatural things. God gave him permission to incite an enemy against Job, send storms to destroy his property, and cause Job to suffer physically—but he was not allowed to take Job's life (see Job 1–2). Satan could give the Gadarene demonic strength to break every chain with which people tried to restrain him, but he could not resist Jesus' authority (see Mark 5:1–13). He could hinder Paul from carrying out some plans (see 1 Thessalonians 2:18), but he could not keep the Church from being planted.

Here is the principle to remember: If God's people trust and obey God, they can live free from the control that Satan would try to gain over them.

God's covenant with His people in the Old Testament can be stated quite simply: *If you trust and obey Me, I will give you the Promised Land, with all its blessings, and I will give you victory over all the attacks of your enemies. If you do not trust and obey Me, I will allow your enemies to conquer you and deprive you of the blessings of the land.*

Today it's a spiritual enemy, but the principle is the same. There are some things Satan cannot do. He cannot drive God out of our lives. He cannot cause us to sin. He cannot tempt us beyond what we are able to bear (see 1 Corinthians 10:13). He cannot penetrate the shield of faith if we know the truth and choose to believe it. But if we are not acting in faith, and if we are not following God's clear directions, Satan can gain a foothold in our lives.

The new covenant of grace is written on our hearts, and we enter into this covenant by faith. At their Passover meal in the upper room before He was crucified, Jesus told the disciples,

If you love me, keep my commands. . . . Whoever has my commands and keeps them is the one who loves me. The one who loves me will be loved by my Father, and I too will love them and show myself to them.

John 14:15, 21

Unbelief and disobedience may not affect our salvation, but they do affect how we relate to our heavenly Father. Satan cannot rob us of being children of God, but he can keep that relationship from glorifying God—and he'll do whatever he can to keep that relationship upended.

Satan's most effective traps are the lies that he can give us knowledge and power. He wants to tempt us with wrong sources for these. Turning to occult practices for power and knowledge is saying, *I don't believe God is going to supply all my needs. I don't believe He has given us "incomparably great power" [see Ephesians 1:19]. That's why I need to try these other things.*

It shouldn't take any special discernment to recognize that such thinking comes from the pit, not from a loving Father. But Satan is a deceiver—not just a liar, but also a very clever liar. He has seduced God's people in every age with his offers of power and knowledge to deal with the circumstances of life.

Satan is still in the business of using his deceptive power in any way he can. He does this in two entirely different ways. The first is to cause people to fear him. He wants to be feared because he wants to be worshiped. If we fear Satan more than we fear God, we elevate his limited attributes above the unlimited attributes of God.

He also wants to intimidate us with his power. Because he is a supernatural spiritual being, Satan can cause those of us who are confined to the time-space world of planet earth to be fearful of him and what he says he can do. He can appear in very threatening forms and intimidate people with visions of objects that create fear. Fallen angels don't have physical bodies and cannot assume bodies, but they can appear in a form visible to humans. Many people have seen demonic figures in a wide variety of situations. The demon does not actually have a physical body, but it does appear that way.

Demons especially like to use this tactic with children. Children can be frightened easily, especially at night. When children report seeing "things" in their rooms, parents often look around and report that there is nothing or no one there. They don't realize that a child may be seeing something—and that they need to pray with their children and for their children's protection!

Satan does not always appear as a fearsome being. In dealing with Christians, he much prefers the "minister of righteousness" disguise. He comes as a friend who wants to help us. He knows that we humans need significance. If we don't find that in our relationship with God, we will seek it elsewhere. An element of significance is a sense of power to do significant things. No one wants to feel like the low person on the totem pole, not lovable, not known, not needed.

In our culture, Satan fosters that kind of thinking negatively about ourselves. In this way, he prepares humans for what are likely to be his next two temptations. He will suggest either self-destruction as an escape from the problem of feeling insignificant, or he will suggest taking power from the wrong source to try to solve the problem.

Jesus made it clear that Satan came to steal, kill, and destroy (see John 10:10), so of course Satan would suggest to people that they kill themselves. Suicide is an epidemic nowadays. It's a leading cause of death among young people, and in the top ten causes of death among people of all ages in our country.

Satan may also offer us power to overcome our circumstances. He appears as a fount of helpful information for how we can gain power. This opens a person to the whole world of the occult. The world of the occult says that there's a supernatural source of power and knowledge other than God—a source that is readily available to anyone who chooses to use it. (Again, remember animism?)

Satan delivers only enough power or information to keep us coming back. And the price of taking from that source will be a bondage in some other part of our lives. Even if it appears to be good, Satan charges very high prices. He just doesn't tell us up front what the price will be. He is the master con artist. He has had many years of experience, and he knows how to work a con!

Because we humans love the "how-to" answers, we may be drawn to the occult because it says that if you know the right things to do, the right words to say, the right formulas to apply, you can get the power or knowledge you are seeking. We are drawn to the how-to-do-it approach. But when it comes to dealing with human problems, anything that does not lead us back to a relationship with the Creator is a trap. He is the Source of all power and all wisdom.

God's Response to the Occult

God told His people as they were about to enter the Promised Land,

> When you enter the land the LORD your God is giving you, do not learn to imitate the detestable ways of the nations there. Let no one be found among you who sacrifices their son or daughter in the fire, who practices divination or sorcery, interprets omens, engages in witchcraft, or casts spells, or who is a medium or spiritist or who consults the dead. Anyone who does these things is detestable to the LORD; because of these same detestable practices the LORD your God will drive out those nations before you. You must be blameless before the LORD your God.
>
> Deuteronomy 18:9–13

Note that God said it was because of the commitment to and practice of these detestable things by the people living in Canaan that He was allowing Israel to drive them out.

Sadly, Israel did not heed the warning God gave them, and they soon began to participate in the evil practices of the Canaanites. When they did, God withdrew His hand of protection and allowed their enemies to defeat them. Both Israel and Judah were taken captive after God's long years of patient waiting and warning.

We are no different—we will be in bondage if we practice what has always been condemned by God.

SIX

Know Your Strategy

When recruits for the armed forces go to boot camp or basic training, they prepare physically and mentally to participate in war. Preparedness is the name of the game.

That principle readily transfers to participation in spiritual warfare. There can be no doubt that the enemies we are up against have years of experience. They have been coached to know what works and what doesn't. We don't want to enter combat without knowing who we are, knowing our King, knowing our enemy, and knowing how to use effective weapons and strategies against the enemy!

Your Spiritual Bulletproof Vest

When spiritual warfare is mentioned, we all think of Ephesians 6:10–13:

> Finally, be strong in the Lord and in his mighty power. Put on the full armor of God, so that you can take your stand

against the devil's schemes. For our struggle is not against flesh and blood, but against the rulers, against the authorities, against the powers of this dark world and against the spiritual forces of evil in the heavenly realms. Therefore put on the full armor of God, so that when the day of evil comes, you may be able to stand your ground, and after you have done everything, to stand.

In this letter to the Ephesians, Paul describes spiritual warfare and is quite specific about the nature of our enemy and the things we need to do to stand against him successfully. First, we must admit that we are in a battle.

Second, we need to recognize that the devil and the fallen angels are the enemy—and not get sidetracked by fighting each other. Paul makes it clear that the real battle is with Satan.

Third, we need to make sure that we wear the right gear. One of the first things that happens in boot camp is the issuing of clothing and equipment designed and field-tested for battle. Paul applies this image to spiritual warfare in particular. He counsels us that once we have put on the full armor of God so that we can stand our ground, we should,

Stand firm then, with the belt of truth buckled around your waist, with the breastplate of righteousness in place, and with your feet fitted with the readiness that comes from the gospel of peace.

Ephesians 6:14–15

These descriptions of our spiritual pieces of armor might better be described to us in terms like *bulletproof vest, riot squad helmet and shield, ammunition belt,* and *combat boots.* These figures of speech help us get a handle on the basic truth. Perhaps the best summary of the armor is in Romans 13:14, where Paul tells us, "Clothe yourselves with the Lord Jesus Christ."

The belt of truth, for example, is clearly Christ, the living Word of God and the expression of truth in the Scriptures. Truth represents our commitment to follow the righteous King's authority. A soldier who doesn't follow orders is a detriment to any army. Too many have the attitude "No one is going to tell me what to do." The Scriptures have strong words for those who rebel against legitimate authority (see 1 Samuel 15:23; Romans 13:1–5; 1 Peter 2:13–14). Christ is Lord, and His truth becomes our marching orders. Without truth, there is no effective plan to confront the enemy.

Many other things hang on the belt of truth—our weapon, our canteen of refreshing water, our mess kit of food, and other items we need in battle. The breastplate / flak jacket / bulletproof vest is our defense against Satan as the "accuser" (Revelation 12:10). If he accuses us of sin and he is right, we simply agree with the Lord about it and receive God's forgiveness (see 1 John 1:9). If the accusation is a lie, we tell the devil to go to the cross and make his claim there! We can live with the assurance that "there is now no condemnation for those who are *in Christ Jesus*" (Romans 8:1, emphasis added). Being clothed with Christ is the secret to victory.

We wear helmets for biking, skating, and hockey, as well as for military and police action. We know how critical it is to protect the brain. Going back to the figure of the brain as computer, if the computer crashes, then nothing else will matter very much. Yet it's not just the brain that matters; it's what goes into the brain. It's how that amazing computer in our head is programmed. If we have learned how to "take every thought captive to make it obedient to Christ" (2 Corinthians 10:5), we are safe from the attacks of the enemy on this vital part of our lives.

Mobility is also a key element in strategy, so soldiers need good shoes. Paul refers to this part of our outfit as "the readiness that comes from the gospel of peace" (Ephesians 6:15). Many things could be said about this, but perhaps the most important is that we must be available to the Commander to be sent wherever and whenever He chooses to send us. Fear is not to control us, only the word of our Leader. We must be ready and willing to go. We must be trained and be ready for our marching orders.

God never asks for volunteers for this war. We are all in it, whether we want to be or not. But He looks for those who are ready to submit their wills to His in every area of their lives so that He can use them to reclaim territory from the enemy. This is another way of saying that He is looking for those who make Christ Lord—those who "put on" the Lord Jesus Christ.

"But," you ask, "I thought this was the gospel of peace. How does that fit with warfare?"

Our spiritual warfare is against the one who robs a person of peace, and the message we bring is the message that brings peace to a troubled soul. The problem is that the enemy doesn't surrender his territory without resistance; we thus have to be prepared to enforce the victory Christ won at the cross whenever we meet this foe. We need to know his tactics and go into the battle dressed in the "whole armor" of God and equipped with the confidence that we are "more than conquerors through him who loved us" (Romans 8:37).

Our enemy's offensive tactics begin with trying to gain a foothold in our lives. Paul speaks of this when he writes to the Ephesians, "'In your anger do not sin': Do not let the sun go down while you are still angry, and do not give the devil a foothold" (Ephesians 4:26–27). Footholds tend to be built on sins of the flesh (like anger and selfishness), occult activity, unforgiveness, and lies. A foothold becomes a means of control in a person's life. A foothold that is not recognized and dealt with quickly becomes a stronghold, a base for further invasion. A *stronghold* may be defined as a "system of lies" that gives the devil power in our lives. That doesn't mean that we become "demon possessed," but that Satan has an established a beachhead from which he can affect other things in our lives.

The James 4:7 Strategy

So what do we do about strongholds? A key passage in learning to deal with them is James 4:7. The context of James 4 is the Christian's struggle with the world, the flesh, and the devil. In verse 7, James says, "Submit yourselves, then, to God. Resist the devil, and he will flee from you." The two key elements in dealing with spiritual strongholds are thus submission and resistance—submission to God, and resistance of the devil.

The primary steps in submitting to God include: (1) confessing any sin or wrong activity in our lives, (2) renouncing the sin or activity, (3) receiving forgiveness for those sins, (4) forgiving those who have wronged us, (5) renouncing the lies we have believed and affirming the truth, and (6) committing ourselves to God's truth as the basis for our lives.

Confession is simply agreeing with God about anything that He calls sin. It means saying, *Yes, God, that was sin.* Having confessed our sin, we need to renounce it. Renouncing means that we recognize why the sin is sinful and condemned by a holy God, and we resolve to turn from it once and for all. Paul wrote to Titus,

> For the grace of God has appeared, bringing salvation to all, training us to renounce impiety and worldly passions and in the present age to live lives that are self-controlled, upright, and godly.
>
> Titus 2:11–12 NRSVUE, emphasis added;
> see also 2 Corinthians 4:1–2

Many years before this was written, Solomon said, "Whoever conceals their sins does not prosper, but the one *who confesses and renounces them* finds mercy" (Proverbs 28:13, emphasis added). We too easily fall into the "sin-confess-sin-confess" cycle. When we sin, we should confess, renounce, and then resist. As we receive forgiveness, we believe that 1 John 1:9 is true: "If we confess our sins, he is faithful and just and will forgive us our sins and purify us from all unrighteousness." There is a sense in which we don't even need to ask for forgiveness; we rather say, Yes, God, that was sin. Thank You that Christ bore the penalty for that sin at the cross. I receive by faith what He did for me.

The second stage of the James 4:7 strategy is to *resist the devil.* How do we do that? Some teach or at least imply that submitting to God is the only kind of resisting we need to do. It's true that sometimes God seems to do all the fighting for us. Those are wonderful times, but God usually allows us to be actively engaged in this warfare. If God did all the fighting for us, we wouldn't need the armor and the weapons we are commanded to put on and use.

Authorized and Equipped

We need to remember that we resist from our position "in Christ." There are no tactics that will rout the enemy when employed by a person operating "in the flesh," that is, in our own strength, wisdom, or ability. When we are in a daily loving relationship with the Lord, we can be assured that we operate with divine authority behind us, and we are armed with the weapons we need in order to press the battle with confidence.

The first weapon we have is the Word of God. This is the truth that nullifies the effect of Satan's primary tactic of deception. It is the light that dispels the darkness of the one who "has blinded the minds of unbelievers, so that they cannot see the light of the gospel that displays the glory of Christ" (2 Corinthians 4:4). It is the Word that is the "sword of the Spirit" (Ephesians 6:17). It is especially the Word as appropriated by us and spoken with trust and confidence. John tells us that the believers under attack by Satan overcame him "by the word of their testimony" (Revelation 12:11). The Scriptures are not magical incantations to be used by just anyone, but when they are used as the testimony of one who is "in Christ" and who has proved the truthfulness of the Scriptures, they become the weapon that causes the enemy to flee.

When you have quoted Scripture, be sure to use praise as a weapon too! Praise from the mouth of the child of God is a form of testimony. It affirms the truth about God and about the victory of Christ. It is claiming victory before the victory is seen or experienced. Satan hates praise. God is "enthroned" on the praises of His people (Psalm 22:3). Praise invites the presence of God, and Satan wants to avoid that at all costs. The psalmist likens praise to a horn—a horn that summons the heavenly army to battle under the command of the Lord of Hosts (see Psalm 148:14). In another place the psalmist says, "Before the 'gods' I will sing your praise" (Psalm 138:1). The image is of looking our enemy in the eye and routing him by singing praise to God, speaking praise, repeating aloud who God is and what He is doing that is worthy of praise.

Prayer is another powerful weapon against our spiritual enemy. In Ephesians 6, Paul tells us to put on the armor, to take up the sword—and then to pray, not fight! Paul sees prayer not just as a weapon, not just as a prelude, but as part of the battle itself. Prayer is often where the "struggle" against the "the powers of this dark world and against supernatural forces of evil in the heavenly realms" is really fought (Ephesians 6:12). This is why prayer can be difficult. Satan knows that if he can keep us from prayer, he can keep us from striking a battle-ending blow against him. People often complain that when they try to pray, their minds wander, they get sleepy, or they think of a dozen other things. Welcome to the war! When you get into the thick of things, where the decisive battle is being fought, you can expect the action to pick up!

Instead of mental wandering, invite God's Spirit to close the door to every voice but His as you begin to pray. Invite God to speak because you are listening. And instead of grunting it out, begin to praise Him for His mercy and grace in helping you listen and carry out His commands. Your focus will shift, God will be glorified, and the enemy will slink away.

Another factor in resisting the devil is the blood of Christ. Revelation 12:11 (NKJV) says of those whom the dragon (the devil) was attacking, "They overcame him by the blood of the Lamb and by the word of their testimony." We need to be careful about using the word *blood* or the expression *under the blood* as if these have power in and of themselves, because God doesn't use magical words or formulas. Yet the Scriptures say that by the blood we are redeemed, justified, cleansed, and made holy (see Ephesians 1:7; Romans 5:9; 1 John 1:7; Hebrews 13:12). By the blood we have confidence to enter the Most Holy Place (see Hebrews 10:19–22). If by faith we lay hold of these blessings, we are in a position to resist Satan's accusations and attacks. More than that, however, we are in a place where we can be part of building Christ's Church around the world—a Church against which Christ promised that the gates of hell could not prevail (see Matthew 16:18 KJV).

One other weapon stands out as essential for successful warfare—the name of Jesus. Again, the Bible makes it clear that this is not a magic word. Acting "in the name" of another person, you first must have an active relationship with that person and be commissioned by that person to act on his or her behalf. If I went around doing things "in the name of the president of the United States," for example, but I had not been commissioned by him to act in his stead, no one would need to pay any attention to my words. The same is true in seeking to act "in the name of Jesus" when resisting the demons. They don't have to pay any attention to the words, either. The seven sons of Sceva discovered this in a painful way (see Acts 19:13–16). Again, it's about the relationship we have with our King, Commander, and Lord. When we are living close to Him, free from separation, in our true identity, we can act in the power of His Spirit on His authority—and see the enemy flee.

We have been commissioned by our Lord Jesus Christ to go into the world and make disciples of all nations, and with that commission comes the authority needed to carry it out. That doesn't mean that we can go anywhere *we* decide to go and assume the authority to act in His name. But when we go where He sends us, we can be assured that we have the authority we need to resist the devil.

This begins in our personal lives and in our homes. Christian parents have the authority to cleanse and pray protection over their home and family. Christians also have the authority to invade territory long held by Satan and to build the Church. We may not cast demons out of the places we go, but through prayer the enemy's power can be bound, and we can minister victoriously in spite of the worst the enemy can do.

Back to the Basics

Soldiers often need to go back and review the basics; so do many Christians. They have heard powerful spiritual teaching at some time, but they have not been putting it into practice. They need a refresher. In this war, we need to be spiritually fit for battle. We cannot afford to think that we are safe if we ignore the devil. Sooner or later, he will take advantage of any weakness we allow. He still comes to steal, kill, and destroy (see John 10:10). But with the proper equipment and with skill in using the weapons we have been equipped with, we can be more than conquerors.

Here is how a pastor's wife described her experience of victory in a letter to me (Neil):

How can I say thanks? The Lord allowed me to spend time with you just when I was concluding that there was no hope for me to ever break free from the downward spiral of continual defeat, depression, and guilt.

Having literally grown up in church and being a pastor's wife for twenty-five years, everyone thought I was as put together on the inside as I was on the outside. On the contrary, I knew that there was no infrastructure on the inside and often wondered when the weight of trying to hold myself together would cause my life to fall apart and come crumbling down. It seemed as if sheer determination was the only thing that kept me going.

When I left your office last Thursday, it was a beautiful crystal clear day with the snow visible on the mountains, and it felt like a film had been lifted from over my eyes. The [song] was playing . . . "It Is Well with My Soul." The words of the song fairly exploded in my mind with the realization that it was well in my soul for the first time in years.

The next day in the office . . . I heard, "Boy, something must have happened to you yesterday."

I have heard the same songs and read the same Bible verses as before, but it is as if I'm really hearing for the first time. There is underlying joy and peace in the midst of the same circumstances that used to bring defeat and discouragement. . . .

Already the deceiver has tried to plant thoughts in my mind and tell me that this won't last; it is just another gimmick that won't work. The difference is that now I know those are lies from Satan and not the truth. What a difference freedom in Christ makes.

One big challenge is to stay battle-ready when we are not involved in combat. Soldiers in an active battle situation know how important mental and physical conditioning is. But in a time of peace, it's easy to become focused on things that have little to do with being a soldier.

The difference between military warfare and spiritual warfare is that we are always in the battle, whether we realize it or not. The difference is that in spiritual warfare, the enemy cannot be seen. Our struggle is not against people with flesh and bones, but against spirits from the realm of Satan. People may well become involved in the struggle as the instruments Satan uses against us, but the real battle is spiritual.

This means that we always need to be battle-ready. There is no such thing as a place where the enemy is not a present threat. The only sanctuary we have is our position "in Christ." We are not helpless victims in this war, but we are told to be always on guard, because we never know when or where the enemy will launch one of his deceptive attacks.

In this essential guide to spiritual warfare, we have confined our discussion to being fit for battle through spiritual preparedness, not to covering some of the more advanced levels of such warfare. Too often, well-meaning believers either try to stay out of the war by ignoring it, or try to get involved at a level for which they are not prepared. For both of these scenarios, the place to begin is with recognizing the real nature of the battle, and then getting the training needed so that we're ready when the Commander calls us to more direct involvement.

Warfare has both offensive and defensive angles. We are told on the one hand to be prepared to defend ourselves against the attacks of the enemy (see Ephesians 6:10–18; 1 Peter 5:8–9). But we are also told to pray "Your kingdom come" (Matthew 6:10). If God's Kingdom is to come, Satan's kingdom must come down (see Matthew 12:26; Colossians 1:13; Revelation 9:11; 16:10). This involves spiritual warfare.

We are also commanded to be part of the invasion of Satan's kingdom. Jesus sends His disciples "into all the world"

(Mark 16:15)—the world over which Satan rules—to bring people "from darkness to light, and from the power of Satan to God" (Acts 26:18). Even today, this Great Commission tells us to go and make disciples (see Matthew 28:18–20). We can do that by crossing the ocean or just by crossing the street, through our witness at work or at school. It can be accomplished through intercession. In any case, you know that Satan doesn't want this to happen, and he will do everything he can to prevent our fruitful participation in any such activity.

Thus, the battle is all around us. We don't first enter the battle when we become involved in some active "ministry." The battle may intensify when we do, but Satan knows that he can prevent ministry involvement if he can keep us from being trained. If we are not prepared, we will probably not want to go; and if we go out of obligation rather than through the clear working of the Spirit of God within us, we will probably become part of the problem rather than part of the answer. Incompatibility among missionaries is a main reason so many quit missions. When this happens, we recognize that there's a spirit at work other than the Spirit of Christ. Two Spirit-led believers are not going to find themselves incompatible. There may be personality differences, but we need each other. When such differences cause us to be ineffective in our ministries, it can only mean that someone's personality is not under the Spirit's control or that someone is not doing things God's way. The result is that Satan smiles in approval.

We saw an example of this when we were asked to minister to a team of believers involved in a potentially productive ministry. There was a great deal of discouragement among the team members, and some had recently left the ministry.

One said, "Why do we have to have an outsider come in to talk to us? We can't even talk to each other civilly!"

It did not take long to discover that there were many things in that ministry that had either been overlooked or had never been looked at through God's eyes. Many there learned for the first time how to get their sense of identity from their relationship to an unconditionally loving God rather than from a dysfunctional family or a dysfunctional ministry team. One leader admitted that he was very defensive and felt threatened in relations with colleagues, rather than being an example of trust and resting in the Lord. We also readily identified occult practices connected with the place of ministry.

As the truth began to replace the deceptions of the enemy, and as individuals began acting on the truth, the result was a report that "we saw interpersonal conflicts and team internal conflicts begin to be resolved." As those involved learned to practice forgiveness and reconciliation based on their renewed relationships with the Lord, the ministry team reported that this was becoming evident even in the way they conducted business meetings and carried on day-to-day operations.

Satan's plan for the Church is to divide, discourage, and destroy. History testifies to the fact that he has all too often been very successful with that strategy. The reason for this is that on the one hand, we have been ignorant of his tactics (see 2 Corinthians 2:11) and on the other hand, we have not been fit for battle. Satan loves to be ignored. That allows him to go about his deceptive work of keeping the Church from marching "like a mighty army," as God intended it to do.

Consider the following testimony we received from a pastor who readily offered to let us share this experience to encourage others:

I . . . began applying your principles to my problems. I realized that some of my problems could be spiritual attacks, and I learned how to take a stand. . . .

I was a deacon and preacher in a small Baptist church. My pastor was suffering from depression and other problems . . . he committed suicide. This literally brought our church to its knees. . . .

The church elected me as their interim pastor. While in a local bookstore I saw a book of yours [Neil's] on Setting Your Church Free. I purchased and read it. I felt with all the spiritual oppression in our church this was the answer. Only one problem—to get the rest of the church to believe. . . .

Slowly, very slowly, the people accepted my messages, and . . . [one of your staff members] led the leaders of our church through the "Setting Your Church Free." The leaders loved it. . . . Six weeks later, I was able to take all the people through the "Seven Steps to Freedom." I really don't understand it, but we were set free from the spiritual bondage of multiple problems. I can't put it in a letter or I would write a book.

During all of this, one of my middle-aged members, who was an evangelist, was set free, learned who he is in Christ, and is back in the ministry. . . . I saw the twin daughters of the deceased pastor set free and able to forgive their father. . . . At one point, one of the twins was contemplating suicide.

This is a new church; God is free to work here!

We are in a battle, whether we want to be or not. The only question is whether we will fight well, poorly, or not at all. Our Commander has provided the best of armor and weapons, yet they will bring victory only when we use them. Don't give the enemy the satisfaction of neutralizing you in this battle.

Dr. Neil T. Anderson is the founder and president emeritus of Freedom in Christ Ministries, which has offices and representatives in forty countries. Dr. Anderson has authored more than seventy books on Christ-centered living, including *Victory Over the Darkness* and *The Bondage Breaker*. He was formerly chairman of the Practical Theology Department at Talbot School of Theology and has five earned degrees, including two doctorates. Dr. Anderson lives in Franklin, Tennessee. Learn more at FICM.org.

Timothy M. Warner, formerly professor and director of doctoral programs at Trinity Evangelical Divinity School, was a lecturer and seminar leader with Freedom in Christ Ministries, where his primary focus was personal issues and cross-cultural ministry. He is the author of several books, including *Spiritual Warfare*. Timothy and his wife, Eileen, made their home near Fort Wayne, Indiana. He passed into heaven in 2022.

NOTES

www.ingramcontent.com/pod-product-compliance
Lightning Source LLC
Chambersburg PA
CBHW030846090426
42737CB00009B/1125